# TILBURY LOOP

## Dr. Edwin Course

MP Middleton Press

*Cover picture: A train for Fenchurch Street leaves Tilbury on 17 May 1947 consisting of LMS compartment coaches headed by LMS No. 2137. The long footbridge linked the railway settlement, built within the triangle of lines, with the outside world. (H.C.Casserley)*

*First Published August 2002*
*Reprinted December 2007*

*ISBN        1 901706 86 9*
              *978 1 901706 86 4*

*© Middleton Press, 2002*

*Design Deborah Esher*

*Published by*
              *Middleton Press*
              *Easebourne Lane*
              *Midhurst, West Sussex*
              *GU29 9AZ*
*Tel: 01730 813169*
*Fax: 01730 812601*
*Email: info@middletonpress.co.uk*
*www.middletonpress.co.uk*

*Printed & bound by Biddles Ltd, Kings Lynn*

# CONTENTS

# INDEX

# ACKNOWLEDGEMENTS

First I would thank those who have contributed photographs, either taken by themselves or from their collections. Their names appear with the captions and I am particularly grateful to Frank Church, the two Casserleys and to Alan Jackson. Dave Brennand and Ian Harden have provided special assistance with the plans.

Godfrey Croughton kindly supplied the ticket copies. Vic Mitchell undertook the general editing and helped with many comments. Laurie Wing prepared the discs for printing and finally, Catherine Course who not only typed the script but also improved it. Norman Langridge kindly read the proof.

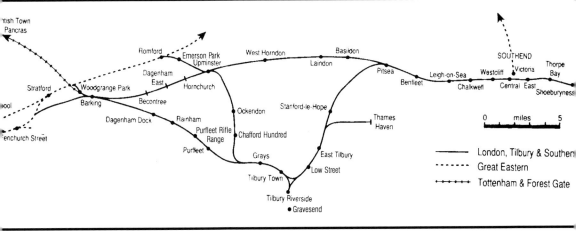

# GEOGRAPHICAL SETTING

The original line for most of the way to Tilbury, traversed level marshland, following the Essex bank of the Thames. There were slight rises at 1 in 150 where the line crossed the rivers Ingrebourne and Mardyke. The only other variations from the level between Barking and Tilbury came where the line intersected spurs of higher ground which came down to the river at Purfleet and at Grays. In each case there were limited earthworks. At Tilbury, the terminal was above the level of the marshes and the platform tracks sloped up to the river bank at 1 in 150.

The extension to Southend ran across the marsh to Low Street beyond which there were slight undulations over the South Essex farmland. A gradient of 1 in 200 came on either side of a peak near Vange, followed by a gentle descent to Pitsea.

The alignment between West Thurrock Junction and Upminster was not influenced by any settlements or gentlemen's estates but ran directly across farmland to the junction with the Southend direct line east of Upminster. At West Thurrock Junction the main line was crossing marshland and the branch climbed onto the higher ground at 1 in 94. It then descended to the valley of the Mardyke, crossed by a 14 arch viaduct, the most impressive engineering work on the route. There were gradients of 1 in 110 each side of the valley after which the line traversed flat fields to Upminster. Beyond there, it diverged from the direct line at the end of a cutting to cross the valley of the Ingrebourne. It continued to Romford across farmland on which the Emerson Park estate was to be built.

The Thames Haven branch ran virtually directly from the main line to the dock site on the river. There was some slightly higher ground at the Stanford-le-Hope end, but for most of its length it traversed marshland. The Corringham Light Railway, having descended from higher ground, ran directly across the marsh to Kynocktown, with no engineering works.

The maps are to the scale of 25 ins to 1 mile, unless otherwise stated.

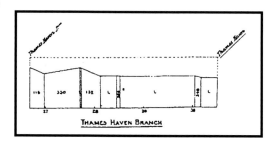

THAMES HAVEN BRANCH

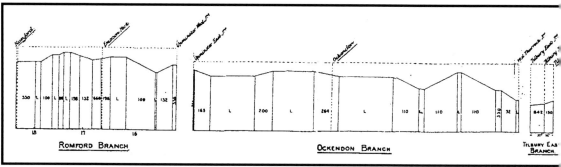

ROMFORD BRANCH     OCKENDON BRANCH     TILBURY EAST BRANCH.

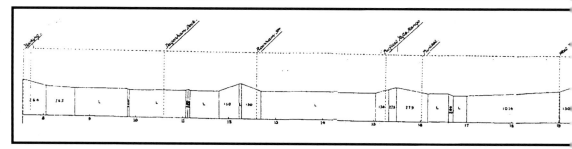

# HISTORICAL BACKGROUND

The Tilbury line was so-called because in its early days, Tilbury was the most important station on the system. However, apart from a few railway houses there was no town there until after the opening of the docks in 1886. In its coat of arms the company displayed London, Kent and Essex with Tilbury represented by the gateway of Tilbury Fort. A better title than London, Tilbury and Southend Railway might have been London, Gravesend and Southend Railway, Gravesend being reached by the company's steamers. The powers of the 1852 Act of Parliament under which the original line was constructed, covered a branch from the Eastern Counties Railway at Forest Gate to the site at Tilbury, with an extension to Southend. Tilbury was reached on 13th April 1854, Leigh on 1st July 1855 and Southend on 1st March 1856. The line was promoted jointly by the Eastern Counties and London and Blackwall Railways, its route including sections of line owned by both of the companies. It competed with the well established paddle steamers and the South Eastern Railway's line to Gravesend and the Kent Coast resorts. Until 1875 it was leased to Peto, Brassey and Betts who hired rolling stock from the Eastern Counties (Great Eastern Railway from 1862). The LTS achieved a degree of independence in 1862, but was not operated as a fully independent undertaking until after the expiry of the lease in 1875. Perhaps more power than was usual lay in the hands of the LTS General Manager. Arthur Lewis Stride was appointed as Resident Engineer and General Manager in 1875 and retired as Chairman when the Tilbury was taken over by the Midland Railway in 1912.

Particularly after the construction of a new direct line via Upminster bypassing Tilbury had been completed in 1888, Southend became a more important source of passenger traffic than Tilbury and Gravesend. However, after the opening of the docks in 1886, the importance of the original line increased for freight traffic. At the London end much of the local traffic west of

Barking (by 1908) and to Upminster (in 1932) came to be carried by underground electric trains. The London, Midland and Scottish Railway absorbed the Midland in 1923 and the Tilbury line became an enclave in LNER territory. Although the promised electrification failed to materialise, at the outbreak of war in 1939 the line had a frequent and reliable service.

After the end of the war in 1945 recovery was slow and at the time of nationalisation in 1948, the former LTS was somewhat run down. In 1949 a logical transfer took place to the Eastern Region of British Railways. Electrification and re-signalling was finally completed in 1962. This fundamental development was followed by a period of little change, and by the 1980s the route was going through another bad patch. Plans for revival were formulated before privatisation on 26th May 1996. Traffic control was to be concentrated on one new centre at Upminster, new trains were to be provided and by 2002 all this had been achieved. The private operator replaced the traditional title of London, Tilbury and Southend line with the less meaningful initials, c2c.

My previous book has followed the line from Barking to Shoeburyness. In this volume we trace the first part of the line to be opened, over the Thameside marshes to Tilbury. We also look at two lines which the LTS might not have chosen to build. The Thames Haven branch of 1855 was taken over as part of a railway to link the Eastern Counties near Romford to a downstream port facility. The line from Grays to Romford, completed in 1893, was a defence line built to protect Tilbury Docks from the Great Eastern. In LTS days these were single track byways and in 2002 they remain the only single track lines on c2c. However, as explained later, both have become more important with the passage of time.

The Upminster to Grays section received electric trains in 1962. The Romford section, after separation from the rest of the route and two threats of closure, was electrified in 1986.

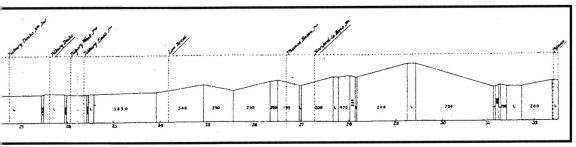

# PASSENGER SERVICES

The line was opened to Tilbury for Gravesend in 1854 with 11 trains a day. The time taken for the 22½ miles varied from 50 to 68 minutes. Use of the steam ferry put an extra 10 minutes on the journey to Gravesend. Until 1875 only First and Second class accommodation was provided but Second class travel on the Tilbury line was cheaper than Third on any other railway. After the completion of the line to Southend in 1856 three, later five, trains were extended to the nascent resort. Initially trains started in two portions, one from Fenchurch Street and one from Bishopsgate to be joined at Stratford, but this ended in 1856. The dedicated boat train services ran in the summer seasons from 1855 until 1880, serving a steam boat from Thames Haven to Herne Bay and Margate. While much of the Gravesend traffic, particularly to Rosherville Gardens was for pleasure because of its lower fares, the LTS did have some residential traffic. In 1856 Gravesend commuters could leave at 7.40am reaching Fenchurch Street at 8.50am. Return was at 4.30pm from Fenchurch Street to arrive at 5.42pm at Gravesend. A report of 1864 noted that the important Gravesend pleasure traffic was declining but the residential traffic was stable. There had been a small increase in the Southend traffic; the service had increased to 6 to 7 trains a day.

In the 1870s and 1880s the great increase was in inner suburban traffic, the number of trains between Fenchurch Street and Barking increasing from 6 in 1875 to 21 in 1883. (These were in addition to the Tilbury and Southend trains). When the direct line to Southend via Upminster was completed in 1885, the route via Tilbury continued to be regarded as the main line. In fact, following an agreement with the Dock Company there were 24 trains a day from Tilbury. (5 up and 4 down were taken off in 1889). Although the route via Tilbury remained important, carrying boat trains and freight traffic, by the 1910s the Southend direct line was the main source of revenue.

As explained, the line from Romford through Upminster to Grays was built as a defence line and in its early days carried little passenger traffic. When the first section between Grays and Upminster was opened in 1892, only seven trains a day were provided. The Romford branch was opened in 1893 and after the opening of Emerson Park in 1909 carried a shuttle service to Upminster to protect passengers from the temptation to use the GE route from Romford. Push pull three-coach trains were introduced in 1934 with 30 trains a day on the Romford branch, 12 going on to Grays and 7 to Tilbury. With the advent of BR there was no incentive to lure passengers away from Romford and the service on the Romford branch declined.

There were no fundamental changes in passenger services in the Midland or in the LMS periods. The timetable for the Summer of 1938 retained the pattern of showing what had become the main line and the loop line services in the one table with just Shoeburyness, Tilbury and Fenchurch Street in heavy print. For the up morning peak it showed 17 trains on the main line, plus 6 via Tilbury and 6 starting from Tilbury. The 8.14am from Tilbury carried a few passengers from Stanford-le-Hope and very few from Gravesend, lured from the Southern Electric by the Tilbury's cheap fares. It ran non-stop from Grays to Barking for transfer to the District line and reached Fenchurch Street at 9.0am. WWII played havoc with Tilbury line schedules. After 1946 the Southend Rail Travellers Association had a significant influence on the timetables. The schedules of 1962, concident with electrification, provided by far the best service ever on the Tilbury line, but confirmed the primacy of the main line. Privatisation came in 1996 and the timetable of 2001 showed two up departures from Tilbury Town via Ockenden in most hours and also two from Grays, via Purfleet.

## ROMFORD, UPMINSTER, TILBURY, and GRAVESEND

| Miles | Down | HOUR | | | | | | | | | Week Days | | | | | | | | | | Sundays | | |
|---|---|---|---|---|---|---|---|---|---|---|---|---|---|---|---|---|---|---|---|---|---|---|---|---|
| — | Romford ..........dep. | | | | | | | | | | | | | | | | | | | | | | | |
| 1¼ | Emerson Park Halt...... | | | | | | | | | | | | | | | | | | | | | | | |
| 3¼ | Upminster 670, 674 {arr. dep. | | | | | | | | | | | | | | | | | | | | | | | |
| 6¼ | Ockendon.............. | | | | | | | | | | | | | | | | | | | | | | | |
| 11¼ | Grays................ | | | | | | | | | | | | | | | | | | | | | | | |
| 12¾ | Tilbury Docks.......... | | | | | | | | | | | | | | | | | | | | | | | |
| 13¾ | Tilbury............arr. | | | | | | | | | | | | | | | | | | | | | | | |
| 14¼ | Gravesend (T. Pier)  ,, | | | | | | | | | | | | | | | | | | | | | | | |

August 1934

February 1961

### Table 16 — ROMFORD, UPMINSTER, TILBURY and GRAVESEND—Second Class only

| Miles | | HOUR | | Week Days | | | |
|---|---|---|---|---|---|---|---|
| — | Romford ............dep. | | | | | | |
| 1¼ | Emerson Park Halt...... | | | | | | |
| 3 | Upminster ............{arr. dep. | | | | | | |
| 6¼ | Ockendon.............. | | | | | | |
| 11¼ | Grays................ | | | | | | |
| 12¾ | Tilbury Town A........ | | | | | | |
| 13¾ | Tilbury (Riverside) ... arr. | | | | | | |
| 14¼ | Gravesend (T. Pier).., ,, | | | | | | |

| HOUR | | Week Days—continued | | | Sundays | | |
|---|---|---|---|---|---|---|---|
| Romford ............dep. | | | | | | | |
| Emerson Park Halt...... | | | | | | | |
| Upminster ............{dep. | | | | | | | |
| Ockendon.............. | | | | | | | |
| Grays................ | | | | | | | |
| Tilbury Town A........ | | | | | | | |
| Tilbury (Riverside) ... arr. | | | | | | | |
| Gravesend (T. Pier).., ,, | | | | | | | |

LONDON TILBURY & SOUTHEND RY
8688
[See Back.]
FENCHURCH STREET to
Fenchurch St            Fenchurch St
LOW STREET
LOW ST                    LOW ST
1s. 5d.        Fare        1s. 5d.
Third Class

LONDON TILBURY & SOUTHEND RY
3278
[See Back.]
FENCHURCH STREET to
Fenchurch St            Fenchurch St
GRAYS
GRAYS                    GRAYS
2s 0d.        Fare        2s 0d.
First Class

London Tilbury & Southend Ry.
DOG TICKET.
140
Purfleet to
FENCHURCH ST.
This ticket must be given up at end of the journey

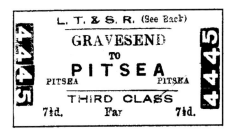

L. T. & S. R. (See Back)
4445
GRAVESEND
TO
PITSEA
PITSEA                    PITSEA
THIRD CLASS
7½d.        Fare        7½d.

# 1. Barking to Tilbury
## BARKING

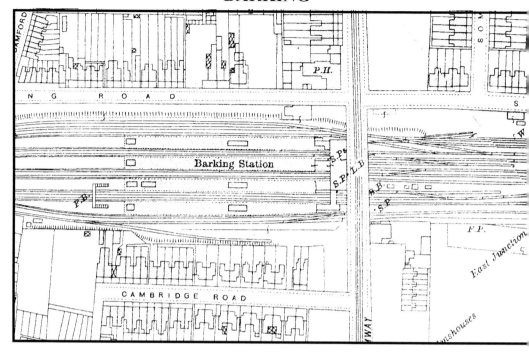

I.     In 1858 Barking was the place at which the cut off line from Fenchurch Street at Gas Factory Junction, joined the original LTS line from Forest Gate Junction on the Eastern Counties Railway. When the direct line to Southend via Upminster of 1888 was built, it diverged at Barking (top right). From 1894 the Tottenham and Forest Gate Railway had joined the original LTS at Forest Gate giving a connection with the Midland Railway. The plan is dated 1915.

1.     A little to the east of the station, the Swedish Lloyd boat train was recorded using the crossing on 12th April 1958. The main line stock was hauled by LMS type 2-6-0 BR no. 43118 built at Horwich Works in 1951. The East Signal Box is visible and construction work had commenced on rebuilding the junction. (F.Church)

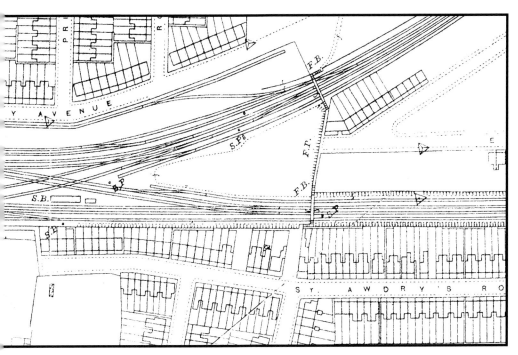

2.	The view taken from the Erkenwald Road Footbridge shows the lines to Tilbury and Southend diverging and the crossover which was used by trains joining or leaving the Tilbury route. It shows Barking East Signal Box and the station buildings of 1908. The DMU is working a temporary shuttle service between Barking and Tilbury on 28th September 1958. (F.Church)

3. A view taken in the early 1950s shows a freight train from the Tilbury direction on the crossing seen in the centre of the previous picture. It consists of an ex-LMS 0-6-0 no. 44071 built by the North British Locomotive Co in 1925 hauling a train of vans. The signal still has semaphore arms, but not for much longer. (H.C.Doyle)

4. Until the construction of the new flyovers west of Barking, trains between St. Pancras and Tilbury crossed over the Southend line on the level. About 1950 a down boat train was recorded on the crossing. The locomotive BR No. 43905 a standard 4F freight locomotive built at Derby was hauling a van for luggage and LMS main line stock in the short lived plum and spilt milk livery. (H.C. Doyle/G.W.Goslin Collection)

5. The seniority of the route to Tilbury was reflected in its following a straight line through Barking in contrast to the divergence of the Southend direct tracks. On 13 April 1958 in connection with the rebuilding of the junction east of the station, the line to Tilbury was being slewed over to the south side of the east Signal Box. The view, taken from the footbridge at the end of Erkenwald Road also shows a steam crane and in the distance the 1908 station buildings and the super cinema of the 1930s. (F. Church)

6. The Tilbury line, in contrast to the later Southend direct line had a number of level crossings. Until its abolition in 1983, for many years the first crossing out of London was over Ripple Road although the signal box was named 'Rippleside'. It was a typical LTS box as supplied by the Railway Signal Co. The finials and barge boards were original but the bricking up of the ground floor windows was a wartime air raid precaution. The crossing gates were operated from the box and a footbridge was provided. The cowls on its underside gave protection from the exhaust of steam locomotives while the high wire fencing sheltered trains from missiles as much as it protected pedestrians. The fine LTS signal post carried semaphore arms indicating which track had been set for running into Barking. The ladder used for changing the parafin oil lamps is on the far side of the metal post. The shot of 28 September 1958 shows chaired track with wooden sleepers. (F. Church)

**Other views of the station can be found in:**
*Fenchurch Street to Barking*
*Barking to Southend*

# RIPPLE LANE

The marshalling of goods wagons on the LTS was carried out at Plaistow and Little Ilford. When pressure increased on these facilities, a new site was selected on flat land available between Barking and Dagenham Dock. Up and down marshalling yards were opened on the west side of what became Renwick Road Bridge in 1940. In connection with electrification and the segregation of the LT lines it was necessary to close Plaistow and Little Ilford and concentrate all marshalling at Ripple Lane. The rebuilding of the two junctions at Barking occupied the yard and so it was closed on 23rd March 1957. The new marshalling yard complete with a hump was designed for the area on the east side of Renwick Road Bridge and was completed between 1958 and 1961. Unfortunately a combination of falling traffic and the increased use of block trains combined to make the new yard superfluous and the hump was closed in 1968. The assorted sidings were replaced by a more modest yard in 1971.

7.    The flatness of the site is shown very clearly in the photograph of 2 September 1957 taken from the Renwick Road Bridge looking towards Barking. From left to right, the double track main line brought into use on 21 July 1957 is followed by the site of the original main line, occupied by a single track and further to the right, the old yard with the goods depot and coal yard beyond. (F.Church)

8.    The view of 5 September 1960 was taken from the Renwick Road Bridge looking towards Dagenham Dock. The hump, to be completed in 1961 is under construction. The up train is on the new up main line, moved into position on 27 May 1960. The post carries the up home signal for Ripple Lane and the distant for Rippleside; there is a hut for the fogman. (F.Church)

# DAGENHAM DOCK

II.　　Dagenham Dock is unique among LTS stations in that it was opened in response to a growth of industry rather than the settlement of people. Whereas many stations were located at the settlement end of the journey to work, Dagenham Dock was at the workplace. Despite the suffix, the dock at Dagenham, in contrast to that at Tilbury, never came to anything. However manufacturing industries developed and in the 1930s the great motor manufacturing complex, including the Ford Motor Co. and Briggs Bodies, was established. Stations such as Westcliff were opened in response to building developers. In contrast, Dagenham Dock was opened in 1908 following advances by Samuel Williams who was establishing industries. Particularly since World War Two workers at Dagenham Dock have motored to their work and the use of the railway station has declined. The plan is dated 1939.

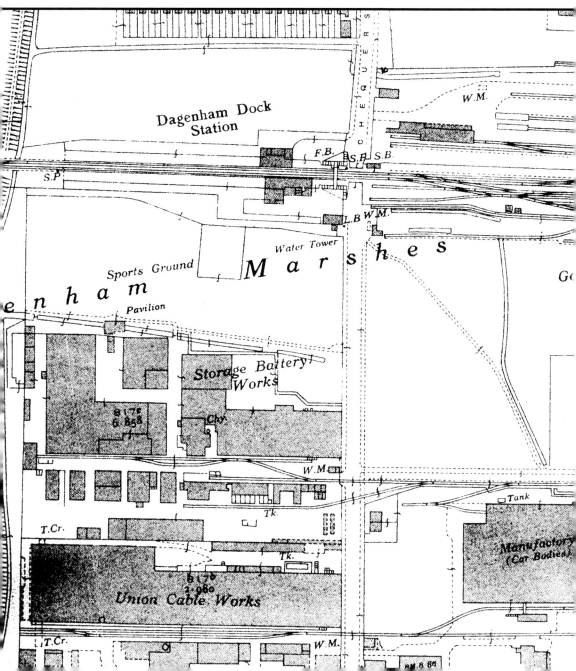

9.    A photograph of 6 June 1959 shows the station virtually unaltered since 1908 and in 2001 it remains probably the least changed station on the LTS. (H.C. Casserley)

10.    This shot of 4 June 1962 shows the provision of electricity for trains and platform lighting but little else has changed.  After electrification, freight and boat trains were diesel hauled and here BR No. D5085 of Class 31 is shown with an Orient Line boat train. (G.W. Goslin Coll.)

11. Dagenham Dock Signal Box with its typical LTS cabin controlled the block section and the level crossing. On 13 April 1958 during engineering work at Barking, a DMU provided a special service between Dagenham and Tilbury. On the left is the side of a diesel locomotive. (F. Church)

12. The view from an up train on 29 May 1990 shows such changes as the replacement of the footbridge for electrification and of semaphores by colour light signals. At the end of the platforms, the running lines separate to run on either side of Ripple Lane Yard. (A.A. Jackson)

13. On 9 March 1957 gas lighting was still in use on the footbridge. The view in the down direction shows the extensive sidings. Those at Dagenham Dock include the Ford Motor Co. The locomotive is BR No. 41989. This was LTSR No. 78 *Dagenham Dock* built by the North British Locomotive Co. in 1908 and withdrawn in 1958. (R.C.Riley)

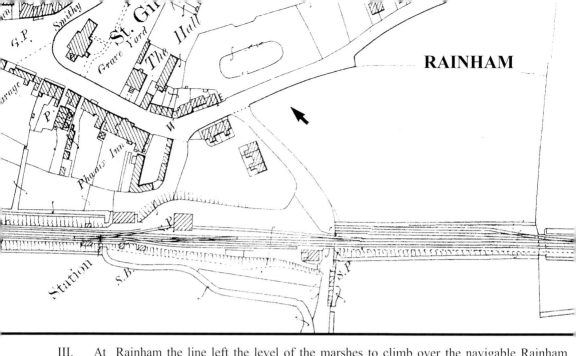

RAINHAM

III.    At  Rainham the line left the level of the marshes to climb over the navigable Rainham Creek.  The district was noted for its market gardening, the traffic being handled both at the station goods depot and at the nearby Wennington Siding.  This was a two-way traffic - market garden produce in one direction and manure, mainly London horse droppings, in the other.  For ease of road access and proximity to the village, Rainham station was sited on an embankment.  It was opened with the line on 1854 but relocated in 1962.  The goods depot was closed in 1965.  The plan shows the station in 1895 before relocation.

14.    Rainham was one of the few LTS stations built of timber - others were Shoeburyness and Thames Haven.  There were a number of  stations with buildings at a higher level than the platforms but Rainham was unusual in having the opposite arrangement.  The original building was destroyed by fire in 1891.  This view of 28 February 1959 shows its replacement. (H.C.Casserley)

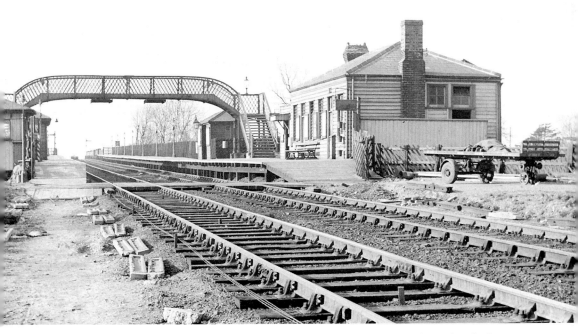

15.     This photograph was taken on 2 March 1958 looking towards London. It shows the platforms, the top storey of the building and a shelter on the right, a booking office of 1914 and shelter on the left, all of timber. The footbridge was second hand, re-erected at Rainham after removal from East Ham in 1907. A trailer to be used with a mechanical horse appears on the right. (F. Church)

16.     We can now enjoy two views taken from the footbridge looking down the line. When the first was taken on 1 September 1958 the original goods depot of 1854 had already been closed to make way for the new station. An extension had been opened previously and this remained in use for goods until 1965. On the right, a length of wooden platform, the 1914 booking office and part of the path leading up to it, and a gas lamp are all visible. By the Ferry Road level crossing is an original LTS crossing keepers cottage of 1854 and a signal box of 1924. The goods yard extension is beyond the level crossing. BR No. 80097 a standard 2-6-4T locomotive is leaving with a train headed by an ex-LNER coach. (F. Church)

17.    The photograph of 11 March 1961 shows work well advanced on the new station. Construction of the concrete platforms and footbridge has commenced together with a gantry for the overhead wires. A steam train is leaving for Tilbury. (H.C. Casserley)

←―――――

18.    The new buildings appear in this view from 12 September 1980. The class 37 diesel was hauling an up freight train consisting of two cement wagons. (A.A. Jackson)

19.    A Class 305 EMU no. 305526 forming the 11.20 Southend Central to Fenchurch Street is shown crossing Ferry Road Crossing on 10 October 1990. Lifting barriers had replaced gates, but the 1924 Midland style box survived until 1996. (M. Turvey)

# PURFLEET RIFLE RANGE

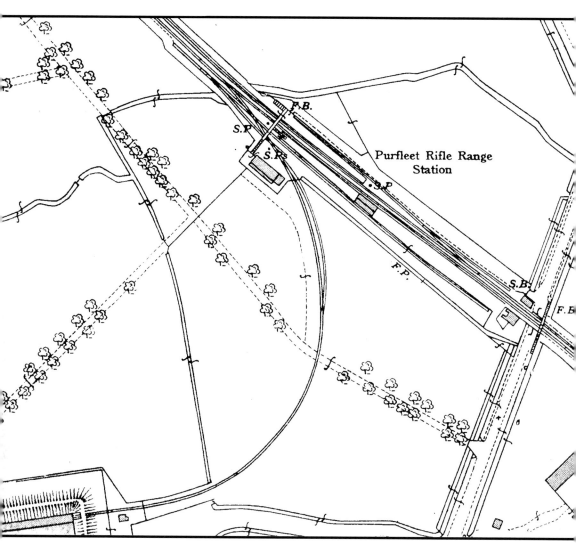

Purfleet Rifle Range
Station

IV.     Four particular types of traffic were associated with Purfleet. First, pleasure seekers visiting
Botany Bay Gardens during the 19th century. Second, freight from the various riverside wharves
including coal and oil. Third, manufactured products such as margarine, soap and cardboard. Fourth,
military traffic particularly associated with the rifle ranges. The plan of 1939 covers the military
traffic including the Rifle Range Station and the War Department Siding.

20.     The photograph of 5 September 1960 shows Ordnance Crossing and includes an LTS crossing keepers cottage of 1854. There was a private siding here from 1863 but, in connection with the opening of the Rifle Range, the War Office applied for a new siding in 1908. This was commissioned in 1909 to be followed by a platform, reserved for military use in 1910. This was slightly upgraded and opened to the public as Purfleet Rifle Range Halt from 1921 until 1948. The signal box of 1910, typical of those supplied by the Railway Signal Co. for the LTS, had the same name as the halt - its predecessor had been called 'Ordnance Crossing'. The halt, the crossing keepers cottage and the signal box have all been demolished. (F. Church)

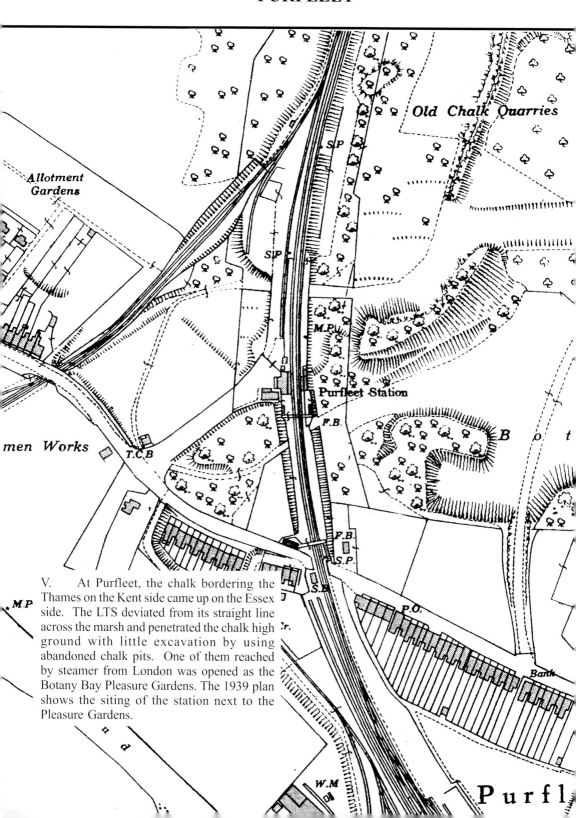

Old Chalk Quarries

Allotment
Gardens

S.P

S.P

M.P.

men Works

T.C.B

Purfleet Station

F.B.

B o t

F.B.

S.P.

S.B.

V.     At Purfleet, the chalk bordering the
Thames on the Kent side came up on the Essex
side.  The LTS deviated from its straight line
across the marsh and penetrated the chalk high
ground with little excavation by using
abandoned chalk pits.  One of them reached
by steamer from London was opened as the
Botany Bay Pleasure Gardens. The 1939 plan
shows the siting of the station next to the
Pleasure Gardens.

M.P

P.O.

Bank

W.M

P u r f l

21.     The main buildings on the up side, were badly damaged by fire in 1903. By this time the traffic to the pleasure gardens had greatly diminished and only a corrugated iron building, perhaps intended as temporary was provided. This was still in use when the photograph of 14 October 1957 was taken and it remained until the station was rebuilt. (H.C.Casserley)

22.     The first signal box was on the station platform, the level crossing being operated from a standard LTS crossing keepers cottage. In 1924 the original box was replaced by a Midland style box situated at the crossing. The photograph of 2 March 1958 shows the 1924 box and the crossing gates with the down starter signal placed low enough to be seen under the footbridge. The down Southend train is hauled by BR no. 42219, a 2-6-4T locomotive built at Derby in 1946. (F.Church)

23.     BR Standard 2-6-4T locomotive runs into Purfleet on a Fenchurch Street to Shoeburyness train of LMS coaches on 23 March 1957. The old buildings and also part of the abutment which carried a mineral line bridge from 1803 to 1840 are visible. The goods depot was not closed until 1964 and wagons are visible beyond the platform. (R.C.Riley)

24.     An unusual notice marking the ownership of the fence at the back of the platform was recorded on 29 March 1959. (F.Church)

25.     Purfleet was a major source of freight traffic. This view of 23 May 1959 shows a coal wharf. (Littlebrook Power Station in the background is on the Kent side of the river). The Thames Board Mills are on the left. An industrial locomotive is to be seen between the water tank and the roof of the signal box. The up train is hauled by BR No. 80136 a 2-6-4T locomotive. It is on one of the few curves on the Tilbury line which carried a speed limit; in this case 35 mph. The curve placed the line in proximity to the wharves and also enabled it to make use of the abandoned chalk pits, reducing construction costs. (F. Church)

26. Another survival at Purfleet was a station seat bearing the LTSR monogram photographed on 20 January 1977. This was probably one of the 90 seats ordered by the LTS in 1885 for £2 each. (E. Course)

27. A view from an up train on 29 May 1990 shows the new footbridge. The signal box survives but the gates have been replaced by lifting barriers and colour lights. The lamp room has gone with the demise of signals with oil lamps. The new station buildings may be seen as a class 59 diesel locomotive approaches on a down stone train. (A.A.Jackson)

# WEST THURROCK JUNCTION

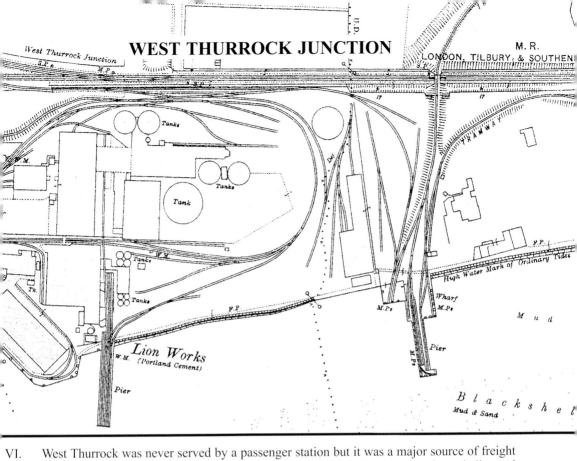

VI.     West Thurrock was never served by a passenger station but it was a major source of freight traffic. From an operating point of view it was the location of the junction between the main line and the branch to Upminster. This was the principal industrial area in South Essex, with the great cement works operating between the 1870s and the 1970s. Their impact on the scene was considerable with a white dust covering everything within some miles of the works. This plan of 1920 is at 20 inches to the mile and continues overleaf. It shows the Grays Works (Brooks) which closed in 1920 and the Lion Works (Wouldham) which closed in 1976.

28.     The first view shows the industrial landscape with an empty stock train passing the BPCM Wouldham or Lion Works on a wet and gloomy day, 29 December 1951. The rotary kiln and the chimneys of the works are visible together with a line of vans which at that time would have carried cement in paper bags. The locomotive is BR no. 41967. (J.H.Meredith)

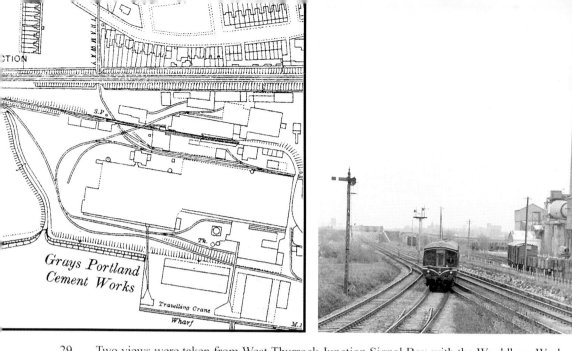

29.   Two views were taken from West Thurrock Junction Signal Box with the Wouldham Works in the right background.  The first from 9 March 1958 shows the junction as opened in 1892.  The home signal has a conventional lower quadrant arm but unusually for the Tilbury line, a concrete post.  The diesel rail car is approaching the trap points. (F. Church)

30.   As part of the resignalling and electrification programme, a third track was laid between Grays and West Thurrock Junction and this appears in the photograph of 8 May 1960.  A new home signal with a metal post has been provided, but the signal on the main line is a colour light.  The open wagons in the cement works siding would have been for coal. No. 80075, a BR standard 2-6-4T locomotive, passes with a train passes for Fenchurch Street via Ockendon. (F. Church)

# THURROCK
# PRIVATE RAILWAYS

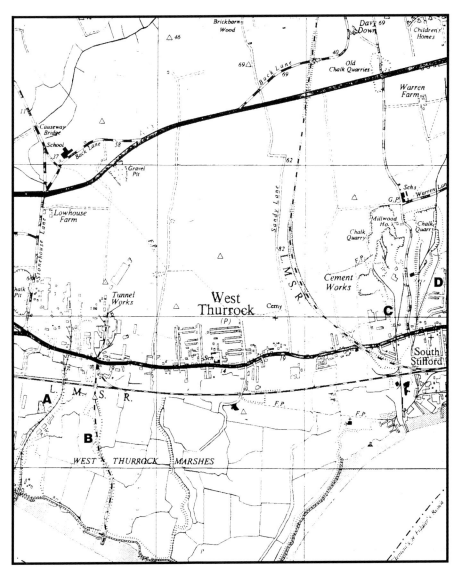

VII.    There were a number of private lines between Purfleet and Grays some with
their main routes running from inland chalk quarries on to cement works and the
main line railway and terminating at riverside wharves.  The map shows four of them.
That of the Thurrock Chalk and Whiting Co. is marked A, and the Tunnel Cement
line is marked B.  C marks the Thames Cement railway and D, that of the Wouldham
Cement works.  The 2½ inch to 1 mile map shows the lines as they were in the 1950s.

31.    Van Den Bergh and Jurgens, producers of Stork Margarine, had a route from their river wharf, serving their works and connected to the main line railway.  They had two fireless locomotives, charged with steam from a stationary boiler. The photograph of 12 July 1952 shows their No. 1 with main line vans running on typical flat bottomed track.  No. 1 was built in 1916 by Andrew Barclay for the Ministry of Munitions at Gretna.  It was purchased in 1919 for the margarine works and is now preserved at the Buckinghamshire Railway Centre. (J.H.Meredith)

32.    The railway of the BPCM Wouldham Works ran between their quarry, the works, the main line and the river.  Most of it was abandoned in the early 1960s and the works was closed in 1976.  The locomotive recorded on 20 January 1951 was *Arab,* an 0-4-0ST built by Peckett in 1899.  The wagons shown were used for conveying chalk from the quarry to the works and were side tippers.  Sheeted over in the background was an Aveling and Porter steam roller. (J.H.Meredith)

33.    The Thurrock Chalk and Whiting Company's railway originally served their quarry, their works, the main line and their wharf.  Other enterprises were established on the line involving  the movement of bauxite, flint and cement.  The various companies closed down and by the early 1980s the system was disused.  The shot of 20 April 1958 shows *Thurwit* an 0-4-0ST, built by Peckett in 1927, hauling main line wagons with works and quarries in the background.  The main line is in the foreground with a heightened embankment and rebuilt bridge to accommodate the overhead wires of the impending electrification. (F.Church)

THURROCK CHALK
& WHITING Cº Lᵀᴰ
QUARRIES

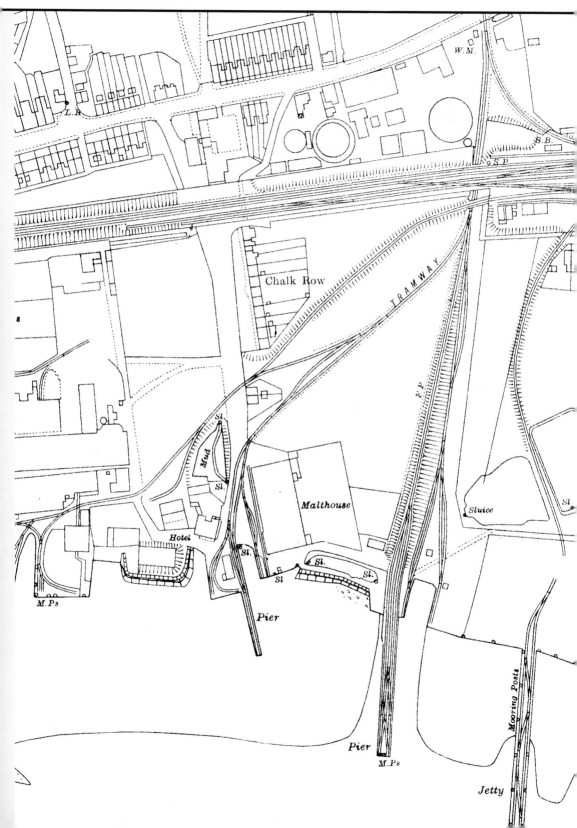

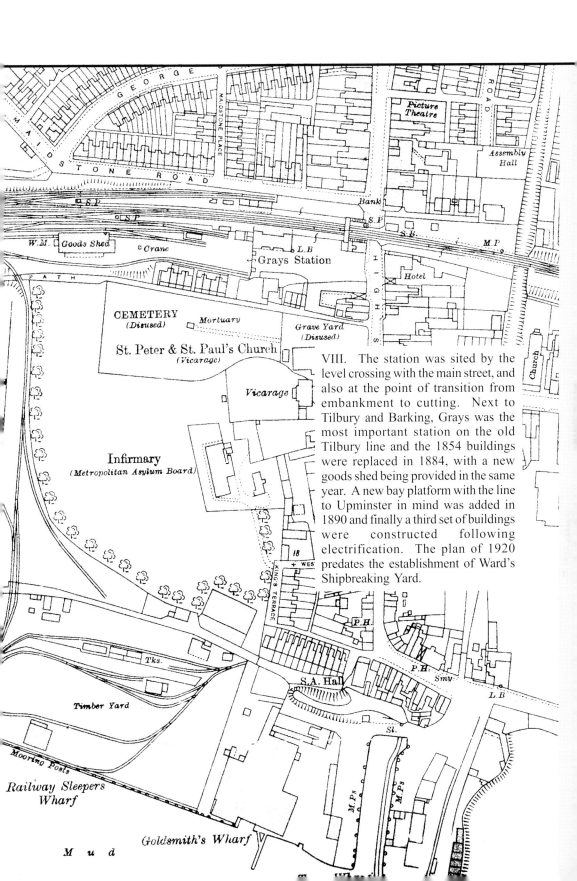

GEORGE

MAIDSTONE PLACE

MAIDSTONE ROAD

ROAD

Picture Theatre

Assembly Hall

S.P.

S.P.

Bank

S.P.

S.B.

M.P.

W.M. Goods Shed

Crane

L.B

Grays Station

Hotel

Church

PATH

CEMETERY
(Disused)

Mortuary

Grave Yard
(Disused)

St. Peter & St. Paul's Church
(Vicarage)

Vicarage

Infirmary
(Metropolitan Asylum Board)

VIII. The station was sited by the level crossing with the main street, and also at the point of transition from embankment to cutting. Next to Tilbury and Barking, Grays was the most important station on the old Tilbury line and the 1854 buildings were replaced in 1884, with a new goods shed being provided in the same year. A new bay platform with the line to Upminster in mind was added in 1890 and finally a third set of buildings were constructed following electrification. The plan of 1920 predates the establishment of Ward's Shipbreaking Yard.

18

WES

KING'S TERRACE

P.H.

P.H.

Smv.

L.B

Tks.

S.A. Hall

Timber Yard

St.

Mooring Posts

M.Ps

M.Ps

Railway Sleepers Wharf

Goldsmith's Wharf

M u d

34. There was a regular boat train working with GER locomotives and coaches which left Liverpool Street for Tilbury on Fridays at 11.30am. On 1st September 1908 the train was hauled by no. 1257 a 2-4-0 of the T26 class (later LNER E4 Class) built at Stratford in 1902 with a 'water cart' type tender. It consists of GE compartment coaches. The train would probably have been

running through to the berth, in which case the main line locomotive would have been replaced by the dock company's locomotive in the Tilbury Dock North Sidings. (K.Nunn/LCGB Collection)

35. The breakdown crane has just arrived on 12th October 1951 to resolve the consequences of a shunting mishap. West Box is in the background. (A.G.W.Garraway)

36.     A photograph of 28 April 1957 shows an up train hauled by BR no. 42678, a 2-6-4T built at Derby in 1945, while a diesel for Upminster waits in the bay platform.  Wagons are visible in the goods yard and a porter is coming down the platform with a trolley to collect parcels traffic left on the platform by the guard of an earlier down passenger train. (F.Church)

37.     An Upminster train stood in the bay platform on 19 September 1956.  It was hauled by BR no. 41977 one of the 4-4-2Ts of LTS design built at Derby in 1930.  The signals provide a contrast, that on the bay platform with a wooden post and a lower quadrant arm while that on the up main has a metal post and upper quadrant arm. (H.C.Casserley)

38. The third set of buildings to be provided on the up side appear in this view of 28 August 2000. Beyond the foot-bridge is the new overbridge which replaced the level crossing. (E.Course)

39. Class 317 set no. 317307 leaves for Fenchurch Street on 7 May 2001. This was a Bank Holiday and the train in the bay platform was operating a service to Barking via Ockendon and Upminster. (M.Turvey)

40. About ¼ mile east of the station was Seabrookes Brewery. This was established in 1799 but did not acquire a private siding until 1884. This view which looks as though it was posed was taken outside the maltings. The locomotive is either no. 49 or no. 50 one of the only two tender locomotives owned by the LTSR. Both were built by Sharp Stewart in 1899 for the Ottoman Railway of Turkey, but were left on the makers hands and were presumably acquired by the LTS at an acceptable price. Seabrooke's sold out to Charrington's in 1929 who, in turn sold the brewery to the Grays Co-operative Society who used it for various purposes. The siding was finally lifted in 1940. (LCGB coll.)

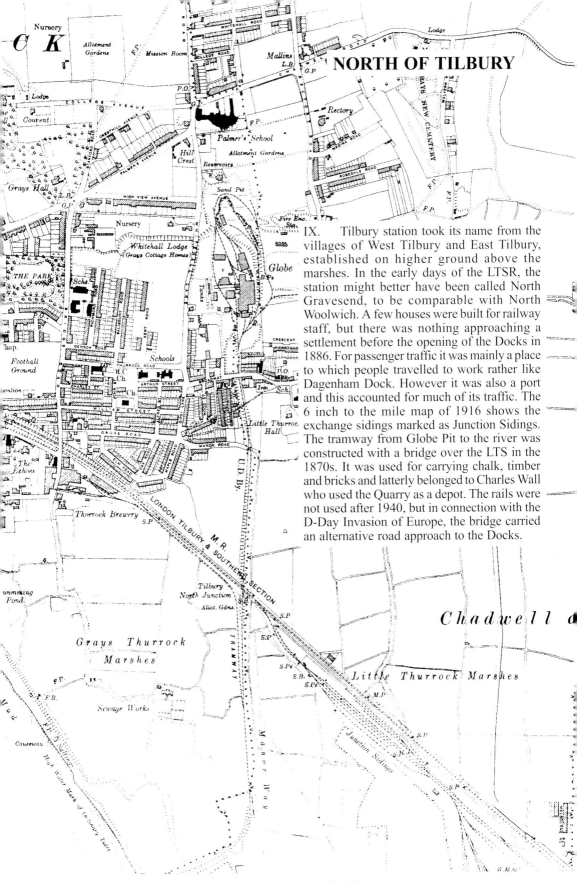

IX.     Tilbury station took its name from the villages of West Tilbury and East Tilbury, established on higher ground above the marshes. In the early days of the LTSR, the station might better have been called North Gravesend, to be comparable with North Woolwich. A few houses were built for railway staff, but there was nothing approaching a settlement before the opening of the Docks in 1886. For passenger traffic it was mainly a place to which people travelled to work rather like Dagenham Dock. However it was also a port and this accounted for much of its traffic. The 6 inch to the mile map of 1916 shows the exchange sidings marked as Junction Sidings. The tramway from Globe Pit to the river was constructed with a bridge over the LTS in the 1870s. It was used for carrying chalk, timber and bricks and latterly belonged to Charles Wall who used the Quarry as a depot. The rails were not used after 1940, but in connection with the D-Day Invasion of Europe, the bridge carried an alternative road approach to the Docks.

41.     The principal rail entrance to the Docks was at Tilbury North Junction, shown in this view of 2 March 1958.  The main line signal box appears on the left and the Port of London Authority Signal Box with its signals are beyond the dockgate. Traffic was exchanged between the main line and dock railways in the North Sidings. The Midland style box replaced the original LTS box of 1886 in 1918. The staff cottages faintly visible to the left of the main line were probably provided for the signalmen. A wooden platelayers hut adjoins the up home signal. (F.Church)

42.     As part of the new works associated with electrification, Tilbury North Junction was abolished and access to the Docks was provided by an extension of Seabrookes Brewery Siding. This shot from a down train taken on 2 October 1990 shows a container train with a diesel locomotive having left the Freightliner Terminal. The staff cottages have been demolished but somewhat remarkably, the platelayers' hut survives.  (A.A.Jackson)

43.     When the LMS and the French Nord railways decided to launch a new continental service, the terminal at Thames Haven having been abandoned, it was decided to use Tilbury. A restaurant car boat train ran from St. Pancras with good connections from the rest of the LMS system.  Owing to lack of patronage in the winter and interference by fog, the service only ran from 1927 until 1932, when it was transferred to Folkestone. The crossing was made at night and so each morning at 7.10a.m. the up boat train ran across the restored level crossing in Ferry Road.  The corresponding down train crossed at 11.15p.m. which accounts for the lack of photographs.  After 1932 the crossing was retained for night use, between 6pm and 6am when the North Junction Signal Box was closed.  It was rarely used and it was remarkable that it survived to be photographed on 1 May 1971. (E.Course)

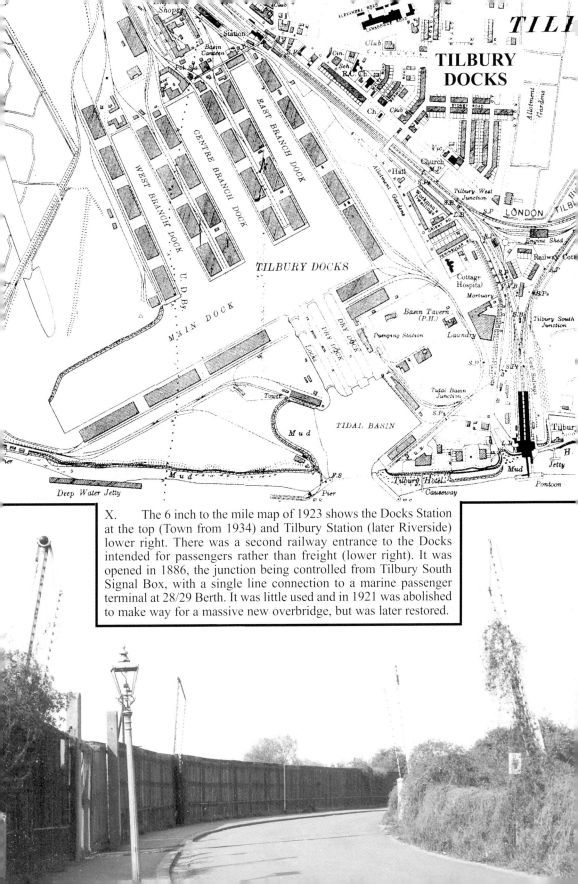

X.     The 6 inch to the mile map of 1923 shows the Docks Station at the top (Town from 1934) and Tilbury Station (later Riverside) lower right. There was a second railway entrance to the Docks intended for passengers rather than freight (lower right). It was opened in 1886, the junction being controlled from Tilbury South Signal Box, with a single line connection to a marine passenger terminal at 28/29 Berth. It was little used and in 1921 was abolished to make way for a massive new overbridge, but was later restored.

44. Although disused since 1st May 1932 and war damaged, something of Tilbury Marine Station remained to be recorded in 1947. It was owned by the Port of London Authority but the building was adapted and leased by the railway company. This is a westward view from a point north of the Fire Station marked in the lower left corner of map XIIb. (Peacock: PLA Railways)

45. This LMS poster was based on a painting by Norman Wilkinson and shows the *S.S.Picard* leaving Tilbury Marine for Dunkirk. The night sailings were operated by two steamers although four were allocated to it. The *Picard* was a 2255 ton vessel built in 1909 for the LNWR/ LYR Fleetwood to Belfast service. (LMS Poster)

TILBURY FOR THE CONTINENT

S.S. 'Picard' leaving Tilbury Marine for Dunkerque

By NORMAN WILKINSON R.I.

LMS

The nightly Tilbury-Dunkerque Service affords connections with all parts of the Continent and is the most convenient Route from the Midlands and North of England to Paris, Basle, Italy, and Central Europe.

46. Before the First World War, vessels destined for the up river docks would anchor off Tilbury and were served by ferry boats and trains from Tilbury Station. For those entering Tilbury Docks, boat trains were run through to the berths, the dock company providing haulage on the dock railway system. This photograph of 20 March 1910 shows the London and India Dock Company's *Nestor*, an 0-6-0ST built by Robert Stephenson in 1907, hauling GER coaches in the Docks. The Port of London Authority had taken over the company in 1909.
(K.Nunn/LCGB coll.)

47.    The same train was photographed at the transit shed.  Passengers passed between the train and the berth through the transit shed - marine passenger terminals were yet to come. (K.Nunn/LCGB coll.)

48.    After the First World War boat trains usually consisted of main line stock and the haulage over the dock railway system was by the main line locomotive. This not only avoided the complication of changing locomotives, but also overcame any braking problems.  A PLA pilotman was carried and the various points and crossings were secured.  The view shows a P&O boat train alongside the transit shed at Berth 33 in 1947. (Peacock: PLA Railways)

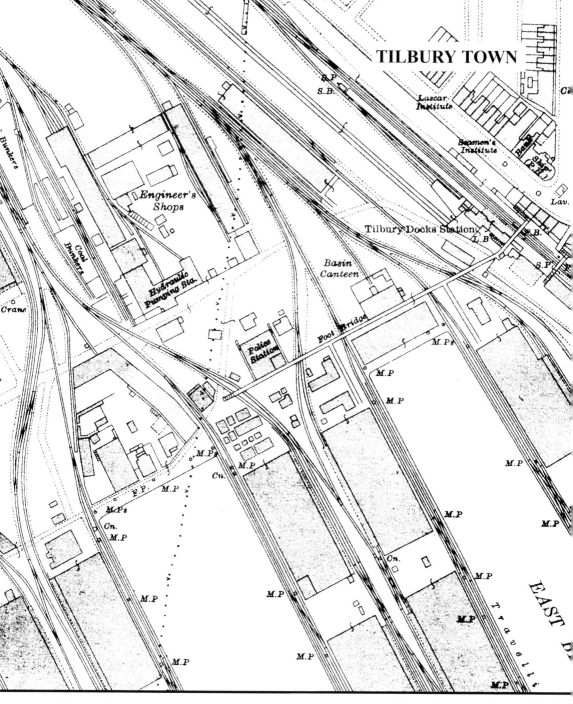

XI.    The plan of 1920 shows the long footbridge linking the station to the docks. Tilbury Docks Station was opened near the main entrance to the Docks when they were completed in 1886. (It had been used in an unfinished state by workmen engaged in dock construction since 1884). It was built by arrangement with the East and West India Dock Company with a guaranteed 'liberal train service'. The station was opened as 'Tilbury Docks' but the centre for the new settlement, as far as it had a centre, adjoined the station so the name was changed to 'Tilbury Town for Tilbury Docks' in 1934. Following the closure of Tilbury Riverside it has become the only passenger station in Tilbury.

49.　　A traditional loose-coupled goods train passed through the up platform on 14 September 1957. The locomotive is 0-6-2T no. 41990, formerly no. 83 of the LTS 69 class, delivered by Beyer Peacock to the Midland Railway in 1912. The station was still lit by gas but the lamp posts bore BR totem type station nameplates. (H.C.Casserley)

50.　　The signal box was replaced by a Midland type box in 1922, and both the goods depot and the signal box were closed in 1961. The view of 28 September 1958 shows a DMU approaching on a special service. (F.Church)

51.    The main buildings on the up side (adjoining the dock rather than town) were in the standard style followed by the LTS in the 1880s. Of the two footbridges, the nearer linked the platforms while the farther ran into the docks. The up train of compartment coaches approaching on 18 July 1959 was hauled by BR no. 80075, a standard 2-6-4T locomotive. (F.Church)

52.    The waiting room and convenience on the down side were in a timber building, hardly up to LTS standards of the time.  When the photograph was taken on 2 March 1958, the run down state may be attributed to the imminence of rebuilding. (F.Church)

53.     The new buildings were opened in 1964.  This shot was taken from an up train entering the station on 29 May 1990.  The buildings are new but somewhat surprisingly it had not proved necessary to rebuild the footbridge to clear the overhead wires.  The long footbridge leading into the dock had been removed. (A.A.Jackson)

54.     By 7 May 2001 the station footbridge had been replaced. The platform had been resurfaced and in addition to the usual whitewash marking its edge, a second yellow line marks the boundary for waiting passengers. The train formed of Class 317 EMU Set No. 317321 is on the stopping service between Fenchurch Street and Southend Central. (E.Course)

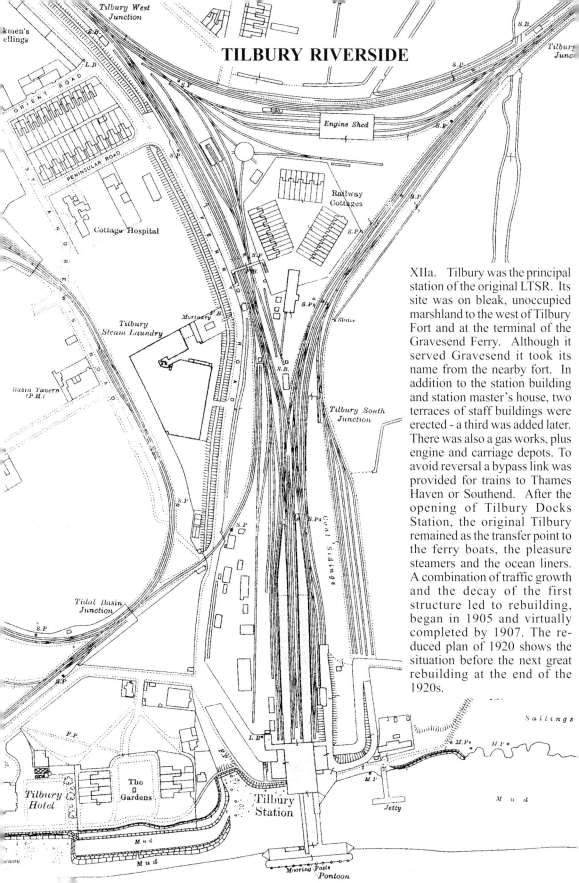

# TILBURY RIVERSIDE

XIIa. Tilbury was the principal station of the original LTSR. Its site was on bleak, unoccupied marshland to the west of Tilbury Fort and at the terminal of the Gravesend Ferry. Although it served Gravesend it took its name from the nearby fort. In addition to the station building and station master's house, two terraces of staff buildings were erected - a third was added later. There was also a gas works, plus engine and carriage depots. To avoid reversal a bypass link was provided for trains to Thames Haven or Southend. After the opening of Tilbury Docks Station, the original Tilbury remained as the transfer point to the ferry boats, the pleasure steamers and the ocean liners. A combination of traffic growth and the decay of the first structure led to rebuilding, began in 1905 and virtually completed by 1907. The reduced plan of 1920 shows the situation before the next great rebuilding at the end of the 1920s.

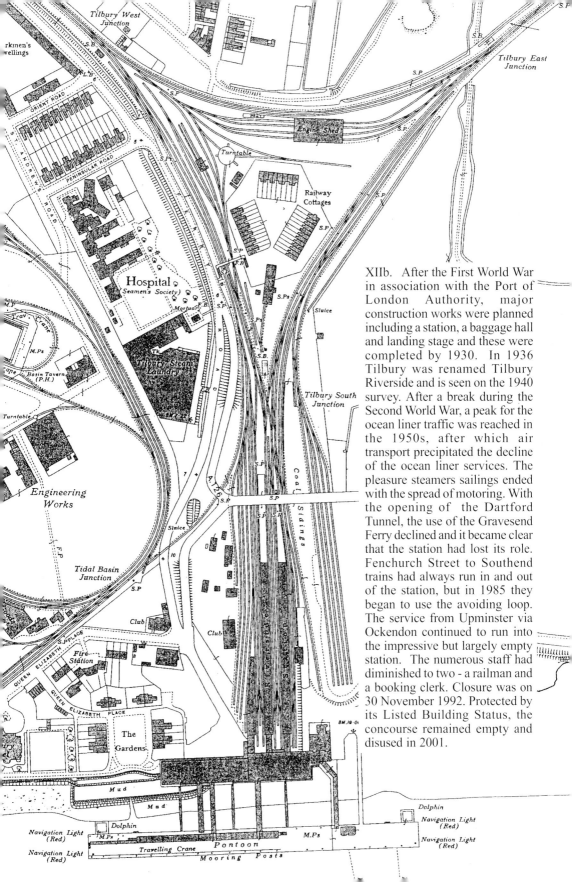

XIIb. After the First World War in association with the Port of London Authority, major construction works were planned including a station, a baggage hall and landing stage and these were completed by 1930. In 1936 Tilbury was renamed Tilbury Riverside and is seen on the 1940 survey. After a break during the Second World War, a peak for the ocean liner traffic was reached in the 1950s, after which air transport precipitated the decline of the ocean liner services. The pleasure steamers sailings ended with the spread of motoring. With the opening of the Dartford Tunnel, the use of the Gravesend Ferry declined and it became clear that the station had lost its role. Fenchurch Street to Southend trains had always run in and out of the station, but in 1985 they began to use the avoiding loop. The service from Upminster via Ockendon continued to run into the impressive but largely empty station. The numerous staff had diminished to two - a railman and a booking clerk. Closure was on 30 November 1992. Protected by its Listed Building Status, the concourse remained empty and disused in 2001.

55. During its active years Tilbury consisted of a triangle with signal boxes at each of the three corners and the terminal station at the south end. When the station was rebuilt in 1906, new signal boxes were constructed at each of the three junctions, all of them surviving until 1961. They were timber boxes with finials and bargeboards in the style to be found in all the boxes supplied by the Railway Signal Company for the LTS at the time. From the London direction trains reached Tilbury West, shown in this photograph of 20 October 1960. The train, hauled by BR no. 80104, is a Fenchurch Street to Southend service, diverted to take the Tilbury avoiding line because of engineering works. To the left of the signal box are "The Dwellings", built for the dock construction workers. (F.Church)

56. Tilbury South box was situated in the fork at the southern end of the triangle. The single track on the left served the southern entrance to the docks, (see picture 43). Beyond the diesel train may be seen the footbridge giving access to the inside of the railway triangle. Part of one of the original terraces is to be seen, with the water tank which was originally fed from the pump at Low Street. The photograph was taken on 2 October 1960. (F.Church)

57.    This view of 18 July 1959 shows Tilbury East box and nos. 42511 and 42503, both from the 1934 batch of 3-cylinder locomotives built for the LTSR. Walkers wait to use the foot crossing. Between the wars, council housing was built in the background. (F.Church)

58.    The new panel box was built to the east of the south junction and was photographed on 2 October 1960, before it was comissioned in 1961. The long overbridge in the background replaced the road crossing under the end of the old station and gave motor access to the new landing stage. In 2001 a new road system was completed and this impressive bridge was demolished. (F.Church)

# Locomotive Depot

59.    From 1854 locomotives were based on Tilbury. The original engine shed was constructed in the south end of the triangle as shown in this view. The locomotives are LTS 4-4-2Ts; that on the left is being coaled manually. The tops of two of the terraces of railway cottages appear, one to the left and one to the right of the engine shed. The coal stack on the right seems to have been protected from theft by a coat of whitewash. Until after the Second World War, the building was used by the Signal Department. (E.Course coll.)

60.    As part of the 1906 upgrading, a new four road engine shed was constructed in the north part of the triangle. For some reason it was built cheaply of corrugated iron which deteriorated so badly that it had to be replaced by corrugated asbestos in 1956. This view of 18 July 1959 shows the shed after refurbishment. At this time, mainly because of staffing difficulties at Plaistow, most of the 2-6-4T locomotives were allocated to Shoeburyness or Tilbury. Tilbury also had some freight locomotives including War Department type 2-8-0s, but no. 90653 shown in the picture was visiting. (F.Church)

61.    The interior is seen in November 1951, with one class 4F 0-6-0 out of steam. At this time five Tilbury 2-6-4T engines (nos. 42218 to 42222) had regular crews and were thus well cared for, attracting praise from regular travellers. The shed was known as a "garage", as it had no workshop, and was much larger than required. It was in deplorable condition, with the smoke hoods in a state of collapse. (A.G.W.Garraway)

62. Although less attractive than the engine shed, the carriage sidings and goods depot were not without interest. For instance there was the body of an LTS Third Class 4-wheeler of the 1880s which was still there to be photographed on 20 October 1957. (F.Church)

63. Rather more exciting was the body of a Midland Railway Pullman Car photographed on the same day. (F.Church)

64. In the goods depot was an ex-Midland coach with its characteristic clerestory roof, also there on 20 October 1957. (F.Church)

# Riverside Station

65. This picture of 8 February 1922 shows the second Tilbury Station of 1907 with the floating pontoon secured in position by dolphins at each end. There are two link spans; a tube for passengers and an open link for livestock and vehicles. On the right the ferry *Carlotta* is at the maintenance depot. (National Railway Museum)

66. The 1907 arrangement with two island platforms with canopies remained virtually unchanged in the 1930 rebuilding. The train at platform 3 has a locomotive in LTS livery running bunker first with a destination board marked 'Fenchurch'. The goods depot is on the left and the carriage sidings on the right. The porter is posed with his trolley and the ladies' dresses would suggest a date of around 1910. (Commercial Card)

67.     This valuable aerial view was presented to guests at the Tilbury Hotel.  It bore the following message - "The Manageress invites you to welcome your friends at Tilbury Hotel when they come ashore.  Restful lounges and comfortable dining rooms with excellent service are at your  disposal. Owned and controlled by the Port of London Authority.   Adjoining Tilbury Passenger Landing Stage".  The view shows the site on the marsh in about 1930.  The foreground is occupied by the jetty on the downstream side of the Tidal Basin of the Docks.  The Dunkirk boat is alongside No. 29 Berth.  Beyond the Hotel and the residences of the dock officials (both built in 1886) are the Baggage Hall and Station of 1930.  The passenger liner looks like a Cunarder and a motor ferry is leaving for Gravesend.  The original ferry terminal and the Fort are in the distance. (A.A.Jackson collection)

68.     But the most exciting thing at Tilbury was the boat trains.  Many trains were boat trains in the sense that they conveyed passengers for the ferry boats or the pleasure steamers, but they were not special as were the ocean liner boat trains.  Before the First World War they consisted of compartment stock and ran from Fenchurch Street, Liverpool Street and St. Pancras.  Some trains ran into the Docks (see pictures 46, 47 and 48) but others used the station for passengers to transfer to liners anchored in the river, using ferry boats.  After 1930, when the landing stage was opened, most trains used the station and passengers walked to join their vessels 'under continuous cover'.  The number of trains per boat depended on the size of the vessel, but in 1933 there was a total of 641 trains. There was a revival in the 1950s.  The last boat train ran from St. Pancras in 1963.  For a while standard electric trains adapted for carrying luggage  ran from Fenchurch Street, but then motor transport took over. This shows a train on arrival on 15 February 1958. The impressive buildings of the station and baggage hall are in the background, as is the funnel of the vessel alongside the landing stage. (F.Church)

69.     Down boat trains ran into the station and after the passengers had left, the train was propelled out of the platform for turning on the triangle.  In the photograph of 18 July 1959, BR no. 43031, an LMS type 2-6-0 built at Horwich in 1949, pushes its empty train out of the platform. (F.Church)

70.     For all the regular shipping lines, boards were provided on the sides of the coaches.  In this shot of 20 October 1957 Coach M 13138 carries a board marked 'London - Swedish Lloyd - Tilbury'. (F.Church)

71.     This is the interior of Tilbury Riverside on 2 October 1990, not long before its closure in 1992. Even in its heyday it only became fully alive when a liner came in. The booking office occupied the centre, the platforms were on the right and the way to the Baggage Hall lay ahead. The space between the two island platforms was filled initially, by a large W.H. Smith bookstall, a kiosk selling confectionery and tobacco and a fruitstall. Beyond the main concourse was another building with refreshment facilities consisting of a First Class Bar, a Third Class Bar and a Dining Room. The provision of staff was lavish, including a full time  railway policeman. The ladders leading to the roof must be a temporary addition. (A.A.Jackson)

72.     When the station closed, the ferry remained open. The railway link was retained by a connecting bus service from Tilbury Town Station. A photograph taken on 7 August 2001 shows the replacement bus. (E.Course)

**Tilbury to Gravesend Ferry**

XIII. There has been a ferry crossing at Tilbury at least since the time of the Domesday Book. At the advent of the LTSR it was in the hands of Gravesend Corporation and the War Department, one in each direction. It was an essential link in the LTS route between London and Gravesend but initially, the company's steamers were authorised to carry railway passengers only. After the end of the leasing period the LTS, by means of lease or purchase, became the sole operator

**GRAVESEND**

73.    The first of the photographs of the steam period shows the *Edith* built and engined by A.W. Robertson of Bow Creek in 1911.  She appears in LTS livery with a black funnel and a plaque bearing the LTS coat of arms amidships.  She had no forward cabin, the space being available for livestock or vehicles and she was known as a 'cattle boat'.  However, after the construction of the special boats for vehicles, she operated with the pasenger vessels.  Manoeuvrability was achieved by the provision of two compound engines driving separate screws.  Operation depended on the wire operated telegraphs which connected the engine room and the bridge.  The steam operated steering gear was at the stern and was driven from the wheel at the centre of the bridge.  The master operated the telegraph and gave his instructions to the helmsman.  Coming alongside the pontoons and avoiding sailing barges required a high degree of skill.  The view from about 1912 shows the station of 1907 with the old landing place marked by the chimney of the stove of the crews' quarters in the bows. (Commercial Postcard)

of the ferry.  When it was well established, between the wars, boats made the five minute crossing every fifteen minutes.  In 1960 the steam ferries were replaced by three diesel vessels.  The decline of the ferry began in the 1960s particularly after the opening of Dartford Tunnel in 1963.  Ownership passed to Sealink then to the Stena Line of Sweden and finally, in 1991, to White Horse Ferries of Swindon.  A measure of the decline in capacity is the difference between 1927 with seven vessels licensed to carry 2500 passengers, and 1992 with one vessel licensed to carry 95.

74.    A view of 5 July 1958 shows the *Rose* alongside the Passenger Landing Stage.  Although not formally opened until 1930, the ferries had been using their end of the pontoon from 1928.  The link span for passengers appears on the left and that for vehicles on the right.  The top of a double deck bus and also the booking hut for motor vehicles are visible to the left of the link span.  The main station hall is in the left background and the ferry maintenance depot appears on the far right.  The *Rose* was built and engined by A.W. Robertson of Bow Creek in London and commissioned in 1901. (A.A.Jackson)

75. The *Catherine,* photographed on 29 December 1951 was also built and engined by Robertsons but was commissioned in 1903. Like her sister ships she was apparently named after female relatives of the directors. The discs on the foremast, replaced by lamps at night, indicated that she was operating across the shipping lane. The emergency steering wheel for manual operation may be seen and was within hearing distance of the master. The radar installation on the starboard side of the bridge was added in 1949. At the same time the oil lamps of the three sister ships were replaced by electric lighting. After their replacement by diesel vessels with the same names the *Edith*, the *Rose* and the *Catherine* were all broken up in Belgium in 1961. (J.H.Meredith)

76. The passenger vessels were sometimes charted for other uses. This included dock cruises but the most important was acting as tenders for liners anchored in the river. Here, the *Catherine* is lying alongside the P&O liner *Mooltan*. The *Mooltan*, 20952 gross registered tons, was built at Harland and Wolf's yard in Belfast in 1923. She is in the P&O livery of black funnel, buff deckwork and a black hull. (LCGB coll.)

# GRAVESEND

77.     This view of 30 June 1956 was taken from the Terrace Pier looking upstream.  At this time the Port of London was still handling many ships and the towing companies kept their larger tugs at Gravesend.  Here tugs of Alexanders are shown at their buoys. The ferry coming alongside the West Street terminal is the *Tessa* built and engined by the Lytham Shipbuilding Company in Lancashire in 1924 and withdrawn in 1964. (A.A.Jackson)

78.     The second ferry to carry road vehicles was the *Mimie* built and engined by Fergusons of Port Glasgow in 1927.  Coal fired with twin screws and two compound engines, she was similar to the other ferry boats.  Whereas the Tilbury side consisted of uninhabited marshland, Gravesend, where the higher ground came down to the waters edge, was an old established town as this picture of 14 September 1957 shows. (R.M.Casserley)

79. The railway companies treated their Gravesend terminals as railway stations as shown in this photograph of 8 February 1922. The LTS acquired the West Street landing place in 1880, constructing a building with a link span and pontoon and, for a while, it carried all the ferry traffic. In 1884 the LTS purchased the Town Pier from Gravesend Corporation and subsequently made this their passenger terminal. All livestock and goods continued to be handled at West Street, although there were limitations. There was a weight limit of 4 tons on the link span and with no crane on the pontoons on either side of the river, there was a general weight limit of 10 cwt. on the goods accepted. However, when the motor ferries began running in 1924, the facilities at West Street were upgraded. Passengers were always carried on the motor ferries, but in 1965 the Town Pier was closed to passengers, and what was by then a passenger service only was concentrated on West Street. Both buildings were demolished and in 2001 only a small booking office survived. (National Railway Museum)

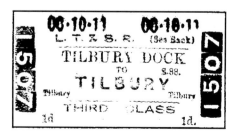

←

80.     The LTSR boundary stone is to be seen at the left of the entrance in picture 79. It was photographed on 1 May 1971. (E.Course)

81.     The Town Pier was constructed for Gravesend Corporation in 1834.  When the railway ferry service began, a floating pontoon was added, but there was no link span and passengers had to negotiate a variable number of stairs and landings, according to the state of the tide.  Unable to reach agreement with the Corporation, the LTS built their own terminal at West Street and withdrew from the Town Pier in 1880.  However in 1884 they purchased it and perhaps influenced by its convenient location at the foot of the High Street, reopened it for passenger traffic, which was handled there until 1965.  The buildings were adapted for office use and the pontoon removed to Scotland.  In 2001 the site was sold for development.  The photograph of 7 February 1922 shows, what was in effect the Gravesend Station of the LTSR. Locomotives did carry destination boards marked 'Gravesend'. (National Railway Museum)

# 2. East of Tilbury
## LOW STREET

XIV. Tilbury Station served Gravesend but originally there was no station to serve East Tilbury and West Tilbury. This was remedied in 1861 by the opening of a station situated between the two which was named after the adjoining hamlet of Low Street. The Board had hopes of freight traffic arising from "the large forts now erecting at East Tilbury". In the event this was the least used station on the LTS and remained virtually unchanged as shown on the plan of 1922.

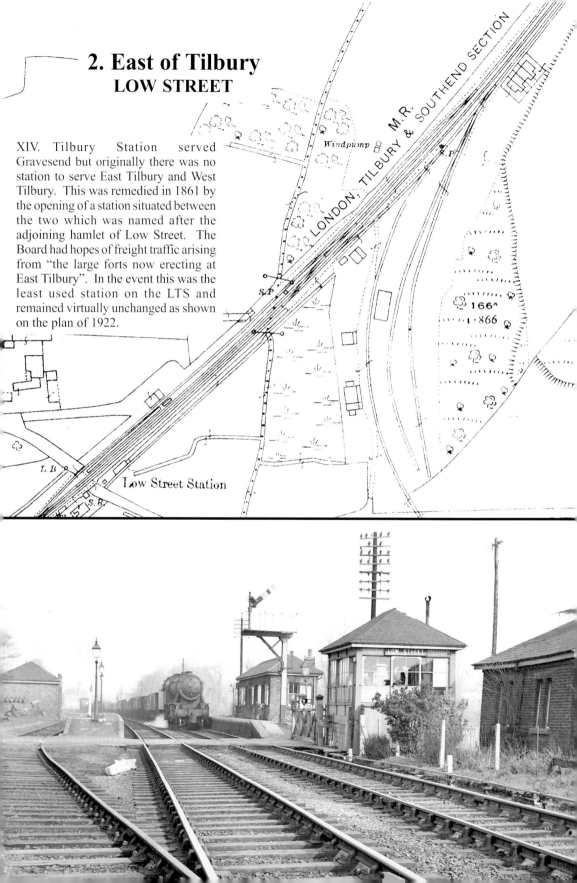

82. The photograph of 23 February 1958 shows the original building on the up side; there was never any building on the down side or any footbridge. Both platforms were originally of the LTS standard length of 200 feet, but to avoid the need for up trains having to stop twice the up platform was lengthened to 530 feet. At electrification, the down platform was lengthened and the oil lamps were replaced by electric lighting. The provision of the goods shed may reflect the hope of military traffic from Coalhouse Fort at East Tilbury; the goods depot was closed in 1964 and the station in 1967. The original crossing keepers cottage of 1854 appears on the right, together with the Midland style box of 1925. The inexplicable placing of a track to the goods yard, necessitated the widely separated gates on the level crossing. Out of sight, was a terrace of four staff cottages reflecting in particular that Low Street was the situation of a well and pump for the water supply for Tilbury, and also a permanent way department siding with a gravel pit, which supplied track ballast. On the up line is WD 2-8-0 no. 90442 with a spoil train. (F.Church)

83. After the closure of the station, the signal box remained to control the well used level crossing until about 1995. By this time all that could be seen was the goods shed and the wicket gate adjoining the level crossing. The photograph taken from the signal box on 3 September 1987 is of special interest as it shows the site of one of very few stations closed on the Tilbury line, and perhaps its most rural. (E.Course)

# EAST TILBURY

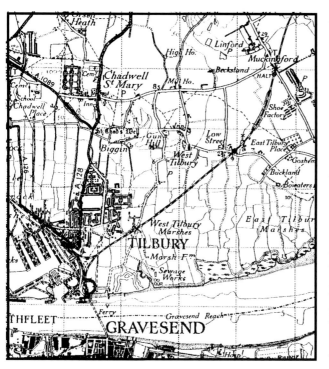

XV. Reference was made in *Barking to Southend* to the building estates in the Laindon and Pitsea area which failed to develop. One of these, with similar rectangular plots was envisaged near Muckingford Level Crossing in 1887. The road system was laid out by 1895 and some houses were built. At first it was called Merrieloots, but by 1900 the name had changed to Linford. A draft agreement for a station was made between the LTS and the developer but, largely on grounds of cost, nothing was done. However in 1932 the Czechoslovakian Bata Shoe Company was responsible for the opening of a new footwear factory, with associated settlement, on a greenfield site on the opposite side of the line to Linford. Although over a mile away from the village of East Tilbury, that place name was used. It is shown on this 1 inch to 1 mile map of 1940.

84.     A halt was opened at the level crossing on 7 September 1936, a mile from Low Street where goods facilities were available. The photograph of 23 February 1958 shows a convenience, a booking office and a shelter on the up side - far more than the facilities usually provided at a halt. Traffic control remained at Low Street Signal Box, but Muckingford Crossing Ground Frame took over the working of the crossing. (F.Church)

85.    This post-electrification view was taken from an up train on 29 May 1990.  The buildings on
the up side have been replaced, but there is still no footbridge nor buildings on the down side.  The
wooden platforms have been replaced with concrete. (A.A.Jackson)

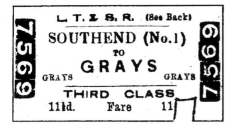

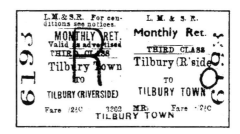

# STANFORD-LE-HOPE

XVI.  Thames Haven Junction dates from the opening of the line in 1855.  The 6 inch to the mile map of 1924 shows the junction, Stanford-le-Hope Station and a detached tramway linking a gravel pit to a wharf.

86. This photograph of 12 October 1957 shows the Midland style signal box of 1927 which lasted until 1973, when control of the junction was transferred to Low Street. Of the two home signals visible, that on the main line has a wooden post and an upper quadrant arm and that on the branch a lower quadrant arm on a metal post. The 12.10pm Saturdays only workmans train is approaching from Thames Haven and the signalman is waiting to receive the token. (F.Church)

87. The arrangement of the platforms at Stanford-le-Hope has altered over the years. Initially the two platforms of the standard LTS length of 200 feet were sited on the north side of the level crossing, with timber buildings on the up platform. During 1880 and 1881 the platforms were extended. The down platform was lengthened to the north, but unfortunately the presence of the goods yard made it impossible to extend the up platform in the same direction. The only possibility was to extend it to the south over the level crossing. This was achieved by mounting the section of platform which crossed the road on wheels, so that it could be moved to permit the passage of road traffic. The photograph taken in about 1909 shows this section and also the roof of the original 1854 building. The photographer was evidently standing just beyond the level crossing and many of the group, mainly of young ladies, are looking at the camera. However, most commendably, a boy is looking in the opposite direction at LTS no. 43 *Great Ilford* of the 37 class. This was built in 1898, rebuilt in 1909 and withdrawn in 1951. (G.Goslin coll.)

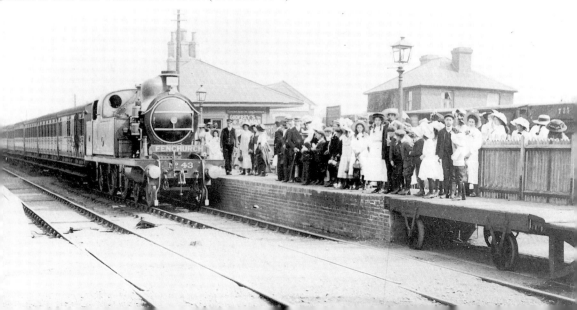

88.     This also shows a view from the level crossing.  No. 38 *Westcliff* of the 37 class built in 1897
is shown in its original condition before rebuilding in 1909.  The train has passed the slotted down
home signal.  The wheeled section of the up platform is on the extreme left.   (Commercial Postcard)

89.     After the original building was destroyed by fire in 1918, a new up platform and building
were constructed on the opposite, south side of the level crossing.  In 1924 the signal box at the end
of the down platform was replaced by a box adjoining the level crossing.  The arrangement with
staggered platforms ended in 1935, when a new down platform was built south of the level crossing
and opposite to the up platform.  This was the arrangement to be seen on 29 May 1990 from an up
train which also shows the new building on the up side.  The signal box had been removed and the
crossing worked with CCTV from 1985. (A.A.Jackson)

# PITSEA

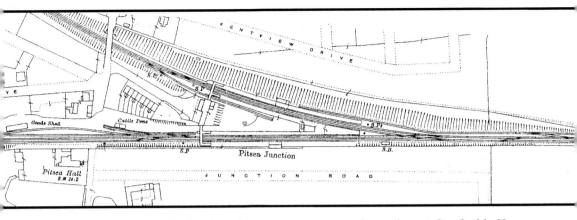

XVII. Just over five miles of rather featurless country separates the stations at Stanford-le-Hope and Pitsea. Pitsea was opened with the rest of the line as far as Leigh-on-Sea in 1855.  In 1888 it became the junction at which the direct line via Upminster joined the original route.  The platforms were slightly re-sited  but the goods yard was virtually unmoved.  The plan is from 1920.

90.     The photograph of 29 December 1957 shows the 1888 station from the Tilbury side.  Details include two cranes and part of the goods yard, which closed on 5th June 1967. A special working is about to use the crossover. (F.Church)

# 3. Grays to Romford

Although the construction of the direct line through Upminster might owe something to the imminence of GER competition for Southend traffic, the only purely defensive line of the LTS was that from Grays to Romford, built to protect Tilbury Docks traffic. It was opened between West Thurrock Junction on the original line and Upminster on the direct line in 1892, and on to Romford in 1893. It was the only single line on the LTS but included a major engineering work in the 14 arch viaduct near Stifford. Initially passenger services were from Romford to Grays or Tilbury but from 1956 the route was divided into two sections. Grays to Upminster was dieselised in 1958 but was included in the electrification scheme. Over the years this section has had more trains from the main line and in 2001 there was an offpeak half hourly service between Southend and Fenchurch Street running via Pitsea, Grays, Ockendon and Upminster. The Upminster to Romford section was operated by diesel trains based on Stratford from 1956, but after two applications for closure was electrified on 1986.

## GRAYS

91. The bay platform at Grays opened in 1890 was always associated with the Upminster route. The photograph of 28 April 1957 was taken when the regular service was worked by steam. However, because of electrification works on this Sunday the service to Upminster was provided by a DMU. The seat incorporated an LTSR monogram; the entrance to the subway was beyond the urinal. (F.Church)

# WEST THURROCK JUNCTION

92.    Three coach push-pull trains with ex-Midland Johnson 0-4-4T locomotives were introduced in 1934.  This view taken in 1953 shows BR no. 58054 (LMS no. 1341) at West Thurrock Junction with the driver collecting the staff for the single line section to Ockendon. (P.Hay)

93.    The driver of a diesel train on a special Sunday service collects the staff on 28 April 1957. (F.Church)

# CHAFFORD HUNDRED

94.     There were extensive housing developments on the line when the London County Council built 5320 houses between 1947 and 1955.  However passengers had to make their own way to Ockendon Station.  This ended when a massive shopping complex was opened in a disused chalk quarry, under the name Lakeside.  In 1995, at the instigation of the developer, a new station named Chafford Hundred (Lakeside) was constructed.  It consisted of a single platform on an embankment with buildings at ground level and direct access to the shopping complex.  The photograph on 28 August 2000 shows the platform and buildings, which were opened to traffic on 26 May 1995. (E.Course)

# OCKENDON

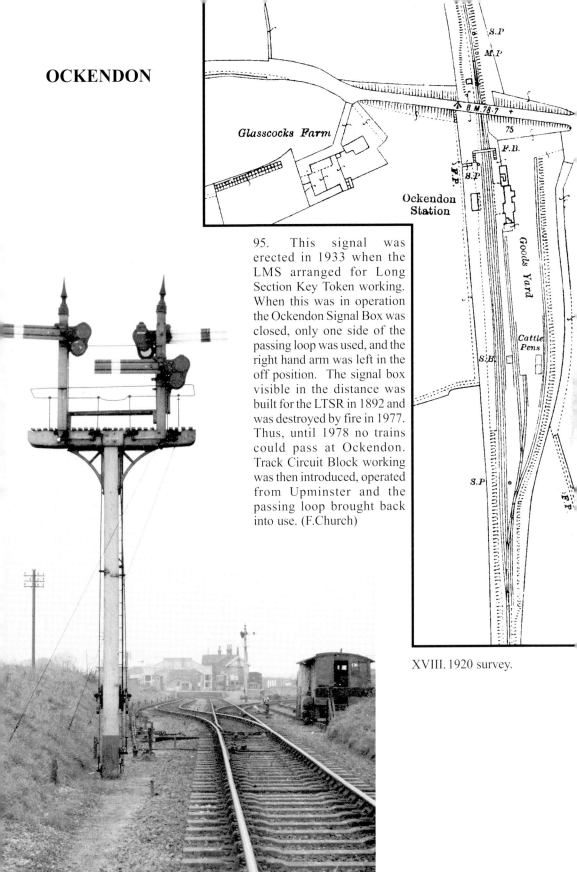

95. This signal was erected in 1933 when the LMS arranged for Long Section Key Token working. When this was in operation the Ockendon Signal Box was closed, only one side of the passing loop was used, and the right hand arm was left in the off position. The signal box visible in the distance was built for the LTSR in 1892 and was destroyed by fire in 1977. Thus, until 1978 no trains could pass at Ockendon. Track Circuit Block working was then introduced, operated from Upminster and the passing loop brought back into use. (F.Church)

Glasscocks Farm

Ockendon Station

XVIII. 1920 survey.

96.    This pleasant view was taken on a Summer's day, 11 June 1938. At this time trains running from Upminster to Grays in a southerly direction were described as up trains. The view is from a three coach push-pull set, hauled by Johnson 0-4-4T locomotive LMS No. 1290. The front of the signal box is visible with a projecting lamp to assist changing the staff at night. Oil lamps line the platform on the down side with the celebrated station garden beyond. (H.C.Casserley)

97.    This northern panorama dates from 29 July 1952. By now electric lighting had been provided and the garden looked as good as ever.   The station was a regular winner of the station garden competition taking special prizes in 1925, 1927 and 1928. (There were only ten special prizes on the whole of the LMS). The station buildings of 1892 are typical of the LTS style at the period. They were still in use in 2001; the goods yard was closed in 1968. (R.M.Casserley)

98.    On the same day, the 5.05pm Tilbury to Upminster train was photographed showing 0-4-4T no. 58038 propelling its 3 coach push-pull set.  With the safety valves lifting, the fireman can afford to enjoy looking at the garden.  The LTS shelter retains its fire buckets, which were probably filled with sand and cigarette ends. (R.M.Casserley)

99.    This view of 9 March 1958 shows how little Ockendon had changed since 1892.  The only obvious changes are to the lighting and to the semaphore signals (but not the signal box).  The footbridge was replaced in 1957 presumably in anticipation of electrification and the signal with co-acting arms was probably erected at the same time.  The passing loop was in use with a down train on the right and an up train on the left.  The goods yard was still in use. (F.Church)

100. This picture of 7 May 2001 shows the same buildings. What has changed is the atmosphere, altered from that of a rural station on a branch line to a much busier station on the main line network. This transition has depended partly on the inclusion of the single line branch in the electrification scheme. This included the rebuilding of the two bridges, relaying of track and consequent raising of the speed limit from 40mph to 70mph. No. 317343 was on the regular interval service between Fenchurch Street and Southend. Signalling is from the new panel box at Upminster. Despite the increased use, doubling is not envisaged. (M.Turvey)

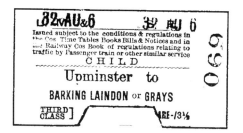

82ᴠAU&6    3ᴠ AU 6

Issued subject to the conditions & regulations in
the Cos Time Tables Books Bills & Notices and in
the Railway Cos Book of regulations relating to
traffic by Passenger train or other similar service

CHILD

Upminster to

BARKING LAINDON or GRAYS

THIRD CLASS ]    ARE-/3½

# NORTH OF OCKENDON

101. This pleasant view from the road bridge at the north end of the station was taken on 17 April 1957. It shows an up train approaching the up home signal. BR no. 69698 of LNER Class N7 was built by Beardmore in 1927 and was transferred to Tilbury in 1955 to work the push-pull sets when the Midland 0-4-4T locomotives were withdrawn. The fencing of wire with concrete posts looks new and may have been part of the general upgrading before electrification. The railwaymens' allotments were a common feature at the time and are using space left for doubling the track. The line between Upminster and Ockendon retains the character of rural South Essex. (B.Pask)

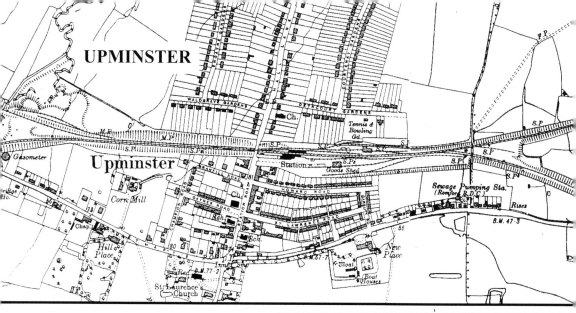

UPMINSTER

Upminster

IXX. This six inch map of 1915 shows the lines from Grays (lower right) and from Romford (upper left).

**The story of Upminster is extensively illustrated in** *Barking to Southend.*

102. This view of 24 March 1956 shows a train from Grays on arrival at Upminster. As illustrated in a previous picture, when the venerable Midland 0-4-4T locomotives were finally withdrawn some ex-LNER locomotives were transferred to replace them. However, if no locomotives fitted for push-pull working were available, any spare engine was pressed into service. Here BR No. 41942 heads the train. (A.A.Jackson)

# EMERSON PARK

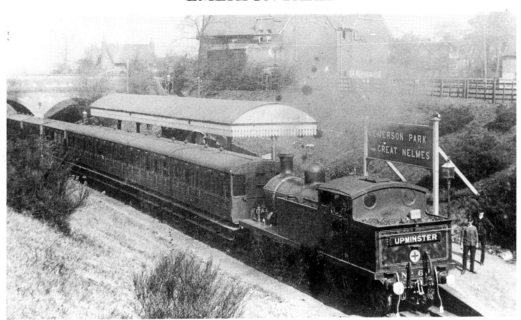

103.　A new estate was opened at Great Nelmes and the two names appeared on the station name board, but not in the timetable.　The train seems to have been specially positioned for this postcard and consists of an LTS 51 class locomotive with LTS compartment stock.　Needless to say, the destination board on the locomotive shows 'Upminster' rather than Romford. (Commercial Card)

104.　There was a modest amount of freight traffic from Romford for the LTS system, at first collected via a connection with the GE and from 1896 from their own depot.　The photograph shows 10.05am train from Upminster to Romford on 8 April 1910.　The locomotive is LTS no. 50, one of two 0-6-0 locomotives built for the Ottoman Railway. (K.Nunn/LCGB Collection)

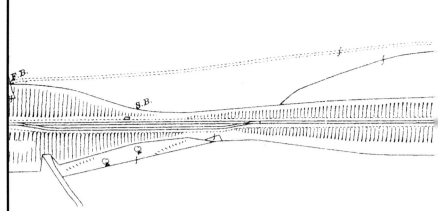

XX.   The plan of 1920 shows the halt and the reversing loop.  The 3¼ mile section between Upminster and Romford was opened as part of the defence route for the protection of Tilbury.  However, it became involved in competition with the Great Eastern for London traffic from the district south of Romford.  Between 1895 and the early 1900s a large estate was opened at Emerson Park, roughly midway between the two lines.  Inevitably there was a demand for a station on the LTS, but the Board hesitated for fear that passengers would use it to travel into Romford and catch trains to Liverpool Street.  Finally in 1909 the LTS opened a

105.   This photograph was taken on 14 February 1976 during the period of diesel operation. The reversing loop had no possible function after the introduction of the push-pull sets in 1934 and was removed about 1936. In 1976 the gas lighting was still intact and was not replaced by electric lights until about 1977. The wooden buildings were prone to damage by vandals and the booking office was burnt down in 1987. (A.A.Jackson)

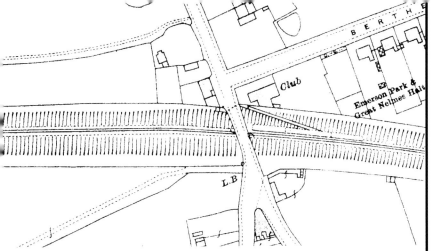

halt at Butts Green called, 'Emerson Park', slightly nearer to Upminster than Romford. A reversing loop (left) was provided west of the halt to enable trains to return to Upminster and thus save passengers from the temptation of using the GE at Romford. However the GE responded by putting on a motor bus service from Emerson Park to Romford which, after the opening of the new station on their line at Gidea Park in 1910, was diverted there from Romford.

106.    The electrification, completed in 1986, was undertaken economically - it will be noted that neither the road overbridge nor the parallel footbridge was rebuilt. When this photograph was taken on 20 April 1994, no. 315810 was forming the 14.00 hours service from Romford. (M.Turvey)

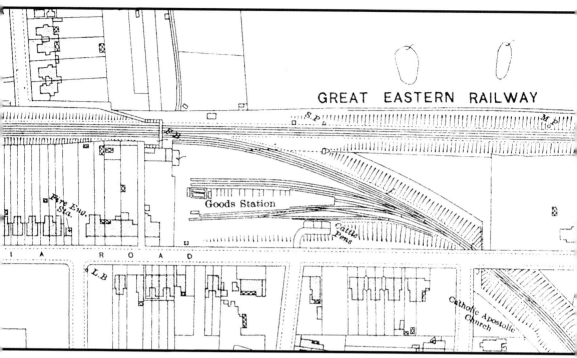

GREAT EASTERN RAILWAY

Goods Station

Cattle Pens

Catholic Apostolic Church

Fire Eng. Sta.

ROAD

LB

XXI. There was no space for a goods depot adjacent to the passenger station and initially the LTS used the GE goods depot. In 1896 they opened their own depot about 1000 yards east of the passenger station as shown on this plan of 1920. From 1955 it handled coal only and was closed completely in 1970.

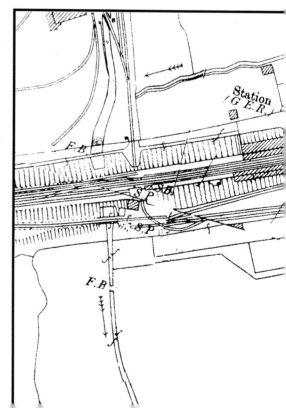

XXII. The plan of 1896 shows the GE goods depot, the GE passenger station and the LTSR passenger station. It also shows the original connection between the LTS and the GE and the LTS signal box. The connection was clipped out of use in 1931 but was restored in 1940. The signal box was replaced by a ground frame in 1936. After the war, the connection was retained and was used by a special train on 27 March 1956. From that year it was in regular use for DMUs coming from Stratford and subsequently for EMUs. It now provides the only access to the Upminster branch.

107. The three storey building at Romford was opened in 1893 and was a one-off, designed to fit the site rather than conform to LTS house style. The postcard shows the canopy over the entrance and footbridge leading to the GE platforms. The building was taken out of railway use in 1934 and access to the LMS platform became via the LNER station. (Commercial Card)

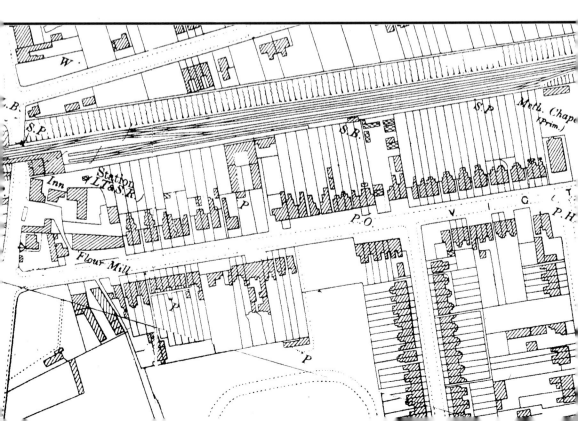

108.    This is the first of five photographs showing the types of train which have served the LTS single passenger platform at Romford.  Taken on 24 August 1929, it shows the 11.44am to Grays hauled by LMS No. 2198.  This had been no. 24 *Ockendon* of the LTS no. 1 class built by Sharp. Stewart in 1884.  (Nos. 19 to 30 were built with snap head rivets instead of the usual countersunk type on the tanks and bunker as shown). The train consists of LTS coaches. (H.C.Casserley)

109.    A view from same point was taken on 13 August 1949, 20 years later.  The train was being worked by one of Johnson's 0-4-4T locomotives, no. 58038 painted in BR livery with one of the push-pull sets.  By this time the LNER line had been quadrupled and resignalled.  The overhead wires are in position and the first electric trains ran from Liverpool Street to Shenfield shortly after this picture was taken.  The only changes on the LMS side are the provision of a new set of wooden planks. (H.C.Casserley)

110.   This view from 15 September 1956 shows one of the LNER locomotives which were used in place of withdrawn Johnson 0-4-4T locomotives.   This was no. 69695 of the N7 class built by Beardmore in 1927.   She was fitted with push-pull gear in 1951 and withdrawn in 1958. (B.Pask)

111.   On 30 March 1968 the only noteable change at Romford was the installation of electric light. The service was being provided by a diesel car stabled at Stratford.   Although unlikely to have been used for many years, the run round for steam locomotives appears to be intact.   An electric train is visible in the former LNER station. (A.A.Jackson)

112. The last of the series was taken on 29 May 1990 and on that day no. 315803 was shuttling between Romford and Upminster. Its passenger carrying capacity far outstripped that of either its steam or its diesel predecessors. The layout has been reduced to a single platform road plus the connection to the main line. The platform was rebuilt with concrete paving in 1989. (A.A.Jackson)

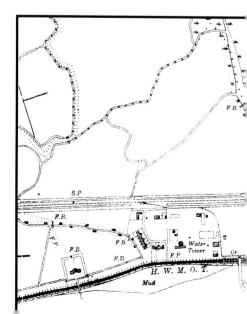

# 4. Thames Haven Branch

XXIII. The Thames Haven line was not a straightforward branch. It began in 1835 with the authorisation of a railway from the Eastern Counties near Romford to a point on the lower Thames where a dock was to be constructed - a kind of downstream Tilbury. Some work was done, but when the LTS was in gestation, the project was in suspense. In the event, the section from Romford to Mucking was abandoned and the Thames Haven line was replaced by a branch from the LTS. This was built and operated by the LTS, although the Thames Haven Dock and Harbour Company lingered until 1861. From 1855 until 1880 the LTS ran regular boat trains each summer season in connection with steamers to the Kent coast, and between 1864 and 1895 there was some freight, mainly livestock. However, in 1886 Thames Haven was eclipsed by the opening of Tilbury. Somewhat unpredictably, failure as a port was followed by success as an industrial centre, first for the manufacture of explosives and then for the oil industry. Explosives manufacture ended after the First World War. Oil peaked in the 1980s after which there was a decline in rail traffic. Oddly enough in 2002 plans were announced for re-using the site of the abandoned Shell refinery as a container port. The six inch map of 1924 shows the original station and the disused cattle pens. The remains of the unfinished dock are to the south of the line and the Shell refinery is yet to be constructed to the north. The London & Thames Haven Oil site is between the track and the shore line. The other end of the branch is shown on map XVI and in picture 86.

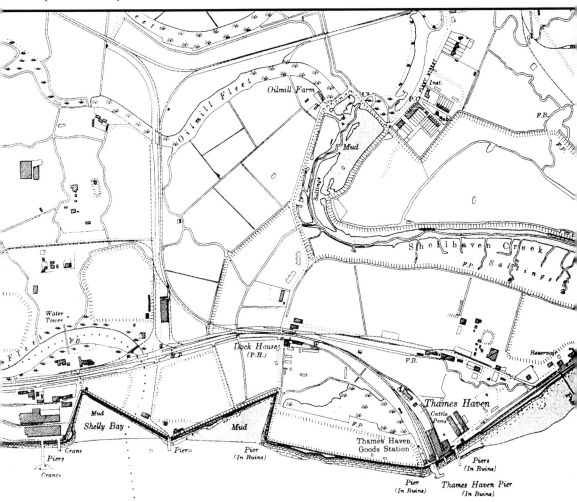

# THAMES HAVEN

113.    The station and pier survived for many years.  There were no regular passenger services after 1880, but it remained open as a goods station, accommodating railway staff until 1953.  A view of it after it was out of use was taken on the occasion of a special train visit on 3 April 1954. The photograph from the river bank shows the original entrance  from the pier, which after a long period of disuse, was abandoned in stages between 1913 and 1922. (E.Course)

114.    This shot from the railway side shows what was left of the train shed and one side of the island platform.  Basically this was as built in 1855 with some reduction and some addition. (E.Course)

115.     After the end of the First World War, both Shell and Mobil built establishments which were much expanded after the Second World War. Typical rolling stock of the 1950s was recorded on the Stephenson Locomotive Society railtour of 3 April 1954. The escalation of traffic did not occur until after the end of petrol rationing and the scene in the early 1950s was virtually a re-run of the late 1930s. The locomotive BR no. 41985 had been LTSR class 69 no. 74 *Orsett* built by the North British Locomotive Co. in 1903 and scrapped in 1959. The tank wagons ran in loose coupled trains. (LCGB Collection)

116.     After the end of the boat trains in 1880, there was no regular passenger service to Thames Haven. With the advent of industry, the railway was used as a highway for pedestrians and cyclists, with the rails used for unofficial trolleys propelled by sails. There was no regular passenger service until 1923. The original terminal was not reopened, but a new platform was built about 200yds west of it. Also three new halts were provided. The service ran on weekdays only from Tilbury, once in each direction. In its early days the train consisted of old LTS 4-wheeled coaches and after they were withdrawn, a mixed collection of vintage stock. This is the last train, the 12.20pm from Thames Haven on Saturday 12 October 1957. Three coaches were provided, one from the North Staffordshire Railway and two from the MR. Ex-LTSR 0-6-2T locomotives were the usual motive power for the workmens train and in this case, BR no. 41992 was provided. (F.Church)

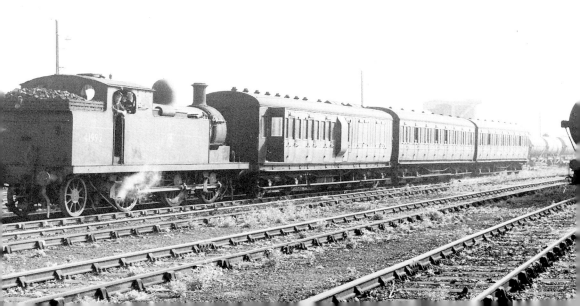

# 5. Corringham Light Railway

XXIV. In time to benefit from the Boer War, Kynocks constructed a large ammunition works on the marshes north of Thames Haven. They built a small settlement, but many of the workers lived in the nearby villages of Corringham and Fobbing. A light railway was constructed between the village and the works, together with a spur which joined the LTS line near Thames Haven. Passenger traffic maximised during the First World War. After it had ended, the ammunition plant was closed and in 1921 Corys acquired the site for oil storage and a refinery. The name of the site including the settlement was changed from Kynocktown to Coryton. During the Second World War the service on the light railway was officially suspended but resumed in 1945. It escaped nationalisation in 1948, but the passenger section was closed in 1952. In 1950 Corys was acquired by the Vacuum Oil Company. In 1956 this became the Mobil Oil Company, which took over the line and upgraded the freight section, which linked the refinery with the Thames Haven branch.

## CORRINGHAM

117.    A party visited the line 17 May 1947 and made a photographic record. This was ex-LTSR third class five compartment coach no.11, built in 1876 and purchased by the CLR in 1915. It had wooden seats and no heating or lighting. Rather surprisingly, Corringham had a brick faced platform which was extended to cope with the long trains of the First World War period. The buildings visible beyond the coach consisted of a waiting shelter, lavatories and a cycle shed. (H.C.Casserley) ⟶

118.    The locomotive shown running round was acquired for the World War I peak traffic in 1917 new from the Avonside Engineering Works, the works no. 1771. The photograph shows the flat bottomed track, characteristic of the line. (H.C.Casserley)

# EAST OF CORRINGHAM

119. An initial descent at 1 in 56 for about quarter of a mile took the train down onto the marsh. The gates at the two level crossings were operated by the fireman. This view shows the special train crossing the Manor Way level crossing. (H.C.Casserley)

# CORYTON

120. The special train terminated here. The station underwent a number of changes and in this view is shown with a shortened platform and no buildings. In the distance is the engine shed and in the headshunt another ex-LTS coach. The original track is still in position but this section of the CLR formed part of the connection between the Mobil Refinery and the Thames Haven branch, and was subsequently relaid to main line standards. Although most of the passenger section is no more, this part of the CLR remains in use as a long private siding for oil traffic. (H.C.Casserley)

XXV. This diagram indicates the complexity of the terminal at Thames Haven. It was used by Shell (UK) until 1993 and subsequently only by Mobil.

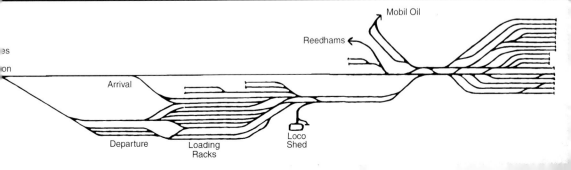

**MP** **Middleton Press**

Easebourne Lane, Midhurst, West Sussex.
GU29 9AZ   Tel:01730 813169

EVOLVING THE ULTIMATE RAIL ENCYCLOPEDIA

www.middletonpress.co.uk   email:info@middletonpress.co.uk
A-978 0 906520  B- 978 1 873793  C- 978 1 901706  D-978 1 904474  E - 978 1 906008

OOP Out of print at time of printing - Please check availability  BROCHURE AVAILABLE SHOWING NEW TITLES